CW00418473

REGIONAL COOPERATION AND INTEGRATION CORPORATE PROGRESS REPORT 2017–2020

ADB SUPPORT FOR REGIONAL COOPERATION
AND INTEGRATION ACROSS ASIA AND THE PACIFIC
DURING UNPRECEDENTED CHALLENGE AND CHANGE

FEBRUARY 2022

ASIAN DEVELOPMENT BANK

Creative Commons Attribution 3.0 IGO license (CC BY 3.0 IGO)

© 2022 Asian Development Bank
6 ADB Avenue, Mandaluyong City, 1550 Metro Manila, Philippines
Tel +63 2 8632 4444; Fax +63 2 8636 2444
www.adb.org

Some rights reserved. Published in 2022.

ISBN 978-92-9269-331-2 (print); 978-92-9269-332-9 (electronic); 978-92-9269-333-6 (ebook)
Publication Stock No. SPR220005-2
DOI: http://dx.doi.org/10.22617/SPR220005-2

The views expressed in this publication are those of the authors and do not necessarily reflect the views and policies of the Asian Development Bank (ADB) or its Board of Governors or the governments they represent.

ADB does not guarantee the accuracy of the data included in this publication and accepts no responsibility for any consequence of their use. The mention of specific companies or products of manufacturers does not imply that they are endorsed or recommended by ADB in preference to others of a similar nature that are not mentioned.

By making any designation of or reference to a particular territory or geographic area, or by using the term "country" in this document, ADB does not intend to make any judgments as to the legal or other status of any territory or area.

This work is available under the Creative Commons Attribution 3.0 IGO license (CC BY 3.0 IGO) https://creativecommons.org/licenses/by/3.0/igo/. By using the content of this publication, you agree to be bound by the terms of this license. For attribution, translations, adaptations, and permissions, please read the provisions and terms of use at https://www.adb.org/terms-use#openaccess.

This CC license does not apply to non-ADB copyright materials in this publication. If the material is attributed to another source, please contact the copyright owner or publisher of that source for permission to reproduce it. ADB cannot be held liable for any claims that arise as a result of your use of the material.

Please contact pubsmarketing@adb.org if you have questions or comments with respect to content, or if you wish to obtain copyright permission for your intended use that does not fall within these terms, or for permission to use the ADB logo.

Corrigenda to ADB publications may be found at http://www.adb.org/publications/corrigenda.

Notes:
In this publication, "$" refers to United States dollars, unless otherwise stated.

Cover design by Josef Ilumin.

CONTENTS

TABLES, FIGURES, AND BOXES

Boxes

PREFACE

The importance of regional cooperation and integration (RCI) for Asia and the Pacific has become even more apparent since the 2017 corporate RCI progress report of the Asian Development Bank (ADB). Global and regional trends, the coronavirus disease (COVID-19) pandemic, and ADB's long-term strategic framework (Strategy 2030) have underscored RCI's crucial role in sustaining the region's resilience, achieving harmonious development, and helping realize the Sustainable Development Goals.

In 2018 and 2019, facing attempts to raise barriers to trade and investment in the global market, many countries in the region worked collectively to establish what soon became the largest regional multilateral trade and investment agreement in the world, the Regional Comprehensive Economic Partnership. ADB's Strategy 2030, published in 2018, identified RCI as one of seven corporate strategic operational priorities. The bank also developed an RCI operational plan for 2019–2024 to design and execute more innovative and ambitious operations reflecting RCI's relevance to many other thematic and sector operational areas.

As the COVID-19 emergency evolved in the region, ADB scaled up its support for countries to cooperate on regional health, trade finance, and supply chains providing essential goods, and to keep borders open to vital merchandise trade. RCI has been important in ADB's overall support to its developing member countries in helping them respond to the COVID-19 emergency, mitigate its impacts, and plan for transition to recovery.

This report highlights the results of RCI operations completed during 2017–2020. It outlines how ADB managed its support for RCI and used its resources, how ADB continued leading development partners in assisting major RCI subregional programs, and the way forward for ADB's RCI over the medium term.

The report aims to contribute to widened interest and participation in and support for RCI, to enable Asia and the Pacific to emerge stronger from the COVID-19 pandemic and advance the region's collective voice in the international community.

The report is the result of a "One ADB" effort by the RCI community and the departments and offices that regularly help implement RCI.

ACKNOWLEDGMENTS

The report was prepared by the Regional Cooperation and Integration (RCI) Thematic Group Secretariat of the Sustainable Development and Climate Change Department, Asian Development Bank (ADB), under the supervision of Ronald Butiong, chief of the RCI Thematic Group. Nguyen Ba Hung, senior regional cooperation specialist, led and coordinated the report's preparation, assisted by Wilhelmina Paz, economist (regional cooperation); Melanie Pre, operations analyst; and RCI Thematic Group consultants Christopher MacCormac, Marinella Llanto Gamboa, and Blessie Marie Santo Tomas, who contributed to data compilation, research, analysis, and drafting of sections of the report.

Other RCI Thematic Group Committee members provided strategic guidance: Xiaoqin Fan, director, East Asia Department; Alain Borghijs, officer-in-charge, Central and West Asia Department; Rosalind McKenzie, principal operations coordination specialist, Pacific Department; Juhyun Jeong, investment specialist, Private Sector Operations Department; Thiam Hee Ng, director, South Asia Department; Alfredo Perdiguero, director, Southeast Asia Department; and Cyn-Young Park, director, Economic Research and Regional Cooperation Department.

Muriel Ordoñez provided publishing support. Rosalie Arboleda provided invaluable administrative support.

ABBREVIATIONS

ADB	–	Asian Development Bank
ADF	–	Asian Development Fund
APVAX	–	Asia Pacific Vaccine Access Facility
ARCII	–	Asia-Pacific Regional Cooperation and Integration Index
ASEAN	–	Association of Southeast Asian Nations
ATTN	–	ADB–Asian Think Tanks Network
BPMSD	–	Budget, People, and Management Systems Department
CAREC	–	Central Asia Regional Economic Cooperation
COVID-19	–	coronavirus disease (previously known as "2019 novel coronavirus")
CPRO	–	COVID-19 Pandemic Response Option
CRF	–	corporate result framework
CWRD	–	Central and West Asia Department
DEfR	–	Development Effectiveness Review
DMC	–	developing member country
EARD	–	East Asia Department
ERCI	–	Regional Cooperation and Integration Division, Economic Research and Regional Cooperation Department
EU	–	European Union
GHG	–	greenhouse gas
GMS	–	Greater Mekong Subregion
HPV	–	human papilloma virus
ICT	–	information and communication technology
IED	–	Independent Evaluation Department
LCY	–	local currency
NTT	–	East Nusa Tenggara
OCR	–	ordinary capital resources
OP7	–	Operational Priority 7
OPPP	–	Office of Public–Private Partnership
PCR	–	project completion report
PRC	–	People's Republic of China
PSM	–	public sector management
PSOD	–	Private Sector Operations Department
RCI	–	regional cooperation and integration
RCIF	–	Regional Cooperation and Integration Fund
RCI-TG	–	RCI Thematic Group
RPG	–	regional public good
SARD	–	South Asia Department

SDCC	–	Sustainable Development and Climate Change Department
SDG	–	Sustainable Development Goal
SERD	–	Southeast Asia Department
SME	–	small and medium-sized enterprise
SOE	–	state-owned enterprise
SPD	–	Strategy, Policy, and Partnerships Department
TA	–	technical assistance
WHO	–	World Health Organization

Note: Data on regional cooperation and integration operations for 2017–2021 were sourced from the Strategy, Policy, and Partnerships Department unless otherwise noted. Data for 2017–2020 are historical. Data for 2021 represent internal projections as of July 2021 that are subject to change consequent to ADB's annual operational programming.

EXECUTIVE SUMMARY

This report succeeds the 2017 Asian Development Bank (ADB) corporate progress report on regional cooperation and integration (RCI) and is the first such report under Strategy 2030.

Against the backdrop of the Asia and Pacific region before the coronavirus disease (COVID-19) pandemic, the report will review 2017–2020 and pandemic-related RCI trends. It will discuss (i) the transition to a new RCI operational plan under Strategy 2030 Operational Priority 7 (OP7): Fostering RCI; (ii) the "One ADB" architecture for implementing OP7; (iii) ADB's RCI operations during the period, including its early responses in 2020 to mitigate the pandemic and its impacts, ease Asia and the Pacific's post-pandemic transition, and initiate recovery; (iv) continuation of ADB's RCI leadership through knowledge and advocacy; and (v) major trends in ADB's support for RCI across the region and organization management of RCI. The report concludes with observations on ADB's RCI performance and a strategic perspective on the way forward.

Context of Regional Cooperation and Integration

Increasingly integrated and complementary Asia and Pacific economy. Intra-regional trade linkages continue to deepen. Economies participate actively in global and regional value chains. Asia leads in the long-term global expansion of most major categories of cross-border flows and in the establishment of new large multilateral regional trade agreements. However, challenges emerging on trade and investment openness were triggering some restructuring of these value chains affecting trade flows.

Mixed COVID-19 impacts on cross-border flows. Trade fell, then rebounded. Tourism imploded and remains weak. Remittances were broadly steady. Intra-regional and external foreign direct investment declined significantly.

New cross-border needs and opportunities generated by COVID-19-induced behavioral trends and expectations. The region's rising economic strength, development, and adoption of new digital technologies; changes in work and business and consumer spending induced by the COVID-19 emergency; and increasing integration are creating new cross-border demands.

ADB's Regional Cooperation and Integration Performance

Performance of RCI operations. RCI results reported in ADB's annual Development Effectiveness Review and independent validation of selected RCI operations point to positive development outcomes.

Plateauing of ADB's RCI loans and grants in the 3 years before the pandemic. By volume and number, the pre-pandemic annual share of RCI projects in total ADB-financed projects remained steady at about 25%.

Transport continued to dominate RCI operations, followed by energy. Some nascent sectors became increasingly visible in RCI operations in health, industry and trade, and finance. The RCI operations within subregions started to advance modestly.

Regional balance. Of ADB's RCI operations, Southeast Asia represented the largest share (35%) followed by Central and West Asia (34%), South Asia (19%), East Asia (5%), and the Pacific (3%). The inter-subregional share stood at 3%, including, among others, projects in high-value agricultural value chains, inclusive finance, and information and communication technology (ICT). Projects involving more than one subregion represented an extremely small share of RCI operations, which is an indication of their challenges, noting the region's trend to expand participation in mega-regional and interregional trade and investment agreements or the need to tackle enormous regional public goods (RPGs) such as mitigating climate change and ocean health deterioration.

Nonsovereign operations. The RCI nonsovereign lending was concentrated in three sectors. Energy captured the bulk, followed by finance, agriculture, and ICT. The share of nonsovereign operations in RCI operations was notable by volume and number; a result that should be reinforced and strengthened going forward, in line with the anticipated increase in private sector cross-border flows resulting from implementation of large trade agreements involving participation of the region's developing countries.

RCI pillar allocation. The RCI portfolio is in the main balanced across OP7's three pillars: connectivity, trade and investment, and RPGs. More stand-alone RPG operations, however, should be pursued in addition to multipillar operations that include RPGs.

Asian Development Fund set-aside for RCI. The Asian Development Fund (ADF) set-aside for RCI has been an important source of financing for RCI operations in developing member countries (DMCs), particularly for the poorest and most vulnerable ones, landlocked countries, fragile and conflict-affected situations, and small island developing states.

Growth and balance of regional cooperation and integration technical assistance. RCI technical assistance has grown in number of projects and expenditure. Sector diversity is strong and RCI is reasonably balanced across OP7's pillars and across subregions, with potential for deepening innovative RCI in traditional sectors and opening up wider opportunities in new sectors.

RCI and ADB's COVID-19 Pandemic Response Option and Asia Pacific Vaccine Access Facility operations in 2020. RCI was incorporated to identify meaningful areas of ADB's technical assistance and investment operations to tackle the outbreak of COVID-19, both on economic measures to mitigate the pandemic's impact, and the public health measures to contain the virus. The RCI components of the COVID-19 Pandemic Response Option and initial Asia Pacific Vaccine Access operations ensured that national responses to COVID-19 were well coordinated and consistent with commitments among DMCs and/or subregional response strategies (e.g., supporting regional trade in medical supplies, small and medium-sized enterprises and small-scale traders in supply chains and livelihoods, supporting easing import processes, strengthening phytosanitary and zoonotic disease detection capabilities and protocols, and procuring vaccines).

Resources and Organization Management Highlights

Regional cooperation and project classification and scorecard. Experience in applying the RCI scorecard has resulted in wider and more systematic dialogue between the RCI Thematic Group (RCI-TG) Secretariat and RCI, sector, and thematic units in ADB's regional departments; more regular and uniform RCI economics training provided to operations staff; and provision of a means to strengthen the link between the results of upstream RCI project preparation knowledge work and the design of new RCI loans and grants.

RCI resource mobilization. The RCI dedicated financing support included RCI special funds under the Regional Cooperation and Integration Financing Partnership Facility, and a significant share of the Asian Development Fund 13 (ADF 13) thematic pool. For the RCI Fund, the review by the Independent Evaluation Department concluded that it achieved its key objective and has potential to promote the RCI agenda further. The fund is aligned with ADB's RCI strategy and related operational plans and has provided additional financing for RCI activities, particularly in cross-border trade facilitation and cooperation on RPGs. For the ADF 13 commitment, in 2020 a total of 29 projects were selected for financing in 2021–2022, totaling $291 million, of which $158 million (54%) was allocated to finance proposals classified as RCI in relation to RPGs.

RCI skills development and acquisition. The RCI-TG Secretariat, in consultation with operations departments and the Budget, People, and Management Systems Department, continues to identify staff skills essential to meet DMCs' current and longer-term needs to resolve COVID-19 and its impacts.

Looking Ahead

Multifaceted RCI situation and outlook. The region continues to face COVID-19 risks, uncertainty, and prolonged adverse socioeconomic impacts and gaps in cross-border health infrastructure and services. But the region is also experiencing greater economic integration, emerging opportunities (e.g., digital trade), and broader expectations for more inclusive and sustainable cross-border development (e.g., portable social protection for economic migrants and sustainable tourism).

ADB's continued support for deeper, wider, and more open RCI toward an inclusive, resilient, and sustainable recovery. The pandemic, while causing enormous development drawbacks, is also an opportunity for DMCs to embark on a more people-centric development path that is inclusive, resilient, and sustainable. This requires countries to work together, which calls for ADB's support for a more expansive RCI agenda—including more sectors, subsectors, thematic areas, and innovation—in consultation with DMCs individually and through ADB-supported subregional and regional cooperation programs. Deeper, wider, and more open RCI will enable DMCs to collectively address the pandemic and post-pandemic socioeconomic and environmental challenges, seize new cross-border development opportunities, and advance the Sustainable Development Goals.

A bigger share and more innovative regional cooperation and integration portfolio. The RCI portfolio should increase as a share of ADB's annual operations in parallel with and to underpin the Asia and Pacific's progress on RCI. An expanding RCI portfolio should contribute toward more and more diverse cross-border flows, the transition to post-COVID-19 recovery, and to bolster ADB's RCI leadership among development partners on the basis of knowledge and innovation, fostering collective action, and financing.

Diversify and enhance RCI skills and strengthen internal and external resource mobilization. Sustaining ADB's RCI leadership (among development partners) and implementing wider, deeper, and more open RCI will require a wider base of quality RCI skills and a maintainable base of financial resources mobilized from within and outside ADB.

Organic Vegetable Value Chains. Farmers growing organic vegetables in Sam Sung Sub-district, Khon Kaen (photo by ADB).

I. INTRODUCTION

The Asian Development Bank (ADB) helps build the global development assistance architecture, which has two main dimensions: a developing country-led and country-focused approach and a regional and global development consensus, with a meaningful portion of development finance provided through regional activities. ADB has a Charter obligation to balance both dimensions and to ensure that they are interdependent and complementary.[1] ADB has three vital roles in regional cooperation and integration (RCI): (i) "honest broker," serving as secretariat and convenor to ease policy dialogue and collective action among countries; (ii) knowledge provider and capacity builder, creating and disseminating knowledge, developing country and institutional capabilities, and advocating Asia and the Pacific RCI in global forums; and (iii) financier, mobilizing project financing. Over the past decades, ADB has demonstrated that its knowledge and technical expertise can provide insights and analysis on regional and global issues and associated implications for national policy making, while its convening ability is key in fostering dialogue among all countries of Asia and the Pacific and harmonizing regional collective action and aid.

This report covers (i) ADB's progress in supporting RCI across Asia and the Pacific during 2017–2020 and (ii) outlook and directions for evolving ADB's RCI operations to meet emerging development needs in the still changeable context of the coronavirus disease (COVID-19) pandemic and global/regional trends. The report was prepared against the backdrop of (i) slowdowns in global and regional trade and investment and a shift to growth centered in Asia and the Pacific, (ii) the imperative of global and regional public goods (RPGs) to protect the environment and humanity, (iii) the dramatic changes in technology that pose significant cross-border opportunities and some challenges, and (iv) the impacts of the COVID-19 pandemic. The report explains how ADB responded to the evolving contexts and assisted the region through RCI activities. The report complements ADB's annual flagship RCI knowledge product, *Asian Economic Integration Report*, by focusing on how ADB implements its strategic operational directions for RCI.

---

[1] Article 1 of the Charter mandates ADB to contribute to the acceleration of economic development of developing member countries, "collectively and individually." Article 2 decrees that "ADB give priority to those regional, sub-regional as well as national projects" to achieve harmonious development. See Appendix 1 for a synopsis of ADB's RCI.

Rural Roads Sector Project in India. Priya Berai, Grade 12 student, studies in a private school and travels by bus from Shekapura to Chandbad. (photo by ADB).

II. MAJOR TRENDS IMPACTING REGIONAL COOPERATION AND INTEGRATION PROGRESS AND BROADER DEVELOPMENT IN ASIA AND THE PACIFIC

Pre-pandemic integration trends. Intra-regional trade linkages continued to deepen across subregions. The linkages were reinforced by pan-Asia RCI initiatives to expand connectivity through multimodal transport. Southeast Asia continues to be the most integrated, while other subregions' performance differs considerably across dimensions (Figure 1). For example, East Asia's integration is strongest with respect to money and finance, infrastructure and connectivity, the regional value chain, and institutional and social integration. However, Southeast Asia outperformed other subregions in trade and investment and movement of people. South Asia and Central Asia trailed other subregions in most dimensions. That said, current initiatives fostering energy trade and improving multimodal transport networks in South Asia are expected to provide explicit benefits and spillover effects for countries in Asia and the Pacific.[2]

Global cross-border flows shifting to Asia and the Pacific. Steady economic growth and investment and advances in technology, but also recent protectionist trends elsewhere, are catalyzing the transition to regional trade integration and supply chain shifts, services sector growth, digitization of business operations, and opportunities for regional enterprise growth. The transition is leading to regionalized business models taking advantage of growing opportunities in the region's commercial, technology, and consumer bases. Digital trade and the services sector are well positioned for cross-border expansion, allowing the creation of growth levers for trade and investment that respond to emerging regional needs (Figure 2).[3]

....

[2]   ADB. 2021. *Asian Economic Integration Report: Making Digital Platforms Work for Asia and the Pacific.* Manila.
[3]   PWC. 2020. *Asia Pacific's Time: We Must Act Now.* November.

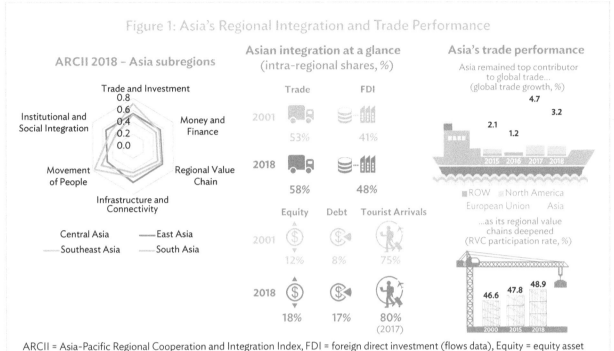

Figure 1: Asia's Regional Integration and Trade Performance

ARCII 2018 – Asia subregions

Central Asia ——East Asia
——Southeast Asia ——South Asia

Asian integration at a glance
(intra-regional shares, %)

	Trade	FDI
2001	53%	41%
2018	58%	48%

	Equity	Debt	Tourist Arrivals
2001	12%	8%	75%
2018	18%	17%	80% (2017)

Asia's trade performance

Asia remained top contributor to global trade...
(global trade growth, %)
2.1 (2015) 1.2 (2016) 4.7 (2017) 3.2 (2018)

ROW North America European Union Asia

...as its regional value chains deepened
(RVC participation rate, %)
46.6 (2000) 47.8 (2015) 48.9 (2018)

ARCII = Asia-Pacific Regional Cooperation and Integration Index, FDI = foreign direct investment (flows data), Equity = equity asset holdings (stock data), Debt = debt asset holdings (stock data), ROW = rest of the world, RVC = regional value chain.

Source: ADB.

Figure 2: Global Cross-Border Flows Shifting to Asia and the Pacific

Global cross-border flows are shifting toward Asia–Pacific

Asia's share of global flow, 2005-07 vs 2015-17,[a] %   2005-07   2015-17

Trade	Capital	Transport		
27 → 33	13 → 23	59 → 62	58 → 64	33 → 36
of global goods flows	of global capital flows	of global container traffic	of global cargo traffic	of global airline revenue

Knowledge	People	Environment	Resources
52 → 65	43 → 48	71 → 70	36 → 43
of patents filed	of international students	of global waste inflows	of global energy demand
25 → 24	33 → 40	Culture	21 → 29
		25 → 38	
of intellectual-property charges	of travelers	of global box-office revenue	of global energy flows

[a] Includes both conventional and renewable energy resources.
[b] In some cases, used alternative periods because of data availability or vitality.

Source: International Monetary Fund, Organisation for Economic Co-operation and Development, UN Conference on Trade and Development, World Trade Organization, McKinsey analysis. McKinsey Global Institute analysis.

Asia – home to the world's largest middle class

The Rise of the Asian Middle Class

Share of the global middle class by region (%)

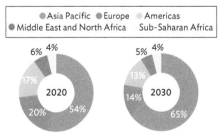

Asia Pacific Europe Americas
Middle East and North Africa Sub-Saharan Africa

2020: 6% 4% 17% 20% 54%
2030: 5% 4% 13% 14% 65%

Middle class = household with incomes between $11-$110 per person/day in 2011

Source: Brookings Institution.

Broadening trade ties among countries of Asia and the Pacific. Countries are taking strategic advantage of their diversity and complementarity by broadening trade ties with each other and to gain market access to other economies outside the region (Figure 3). The Comprehensive and Progressive Trans-Pacific Partnership Agreement came into force in December 2018. It is a mega trade deal composed of 11 economies representing almost 5 billion people. The agreement's parties have a combined gross domestic product of $13.5 trillion. The Regional Comprehensive Economic Partnership, signed in November 2020, includes all 10 countries from the Association of Southeast Asian Nations (ASEAN) plus Australia, Japan, New Zealand, the People's Republic of China (PRC), and the Republic of Korea, representing Asia and the Pacific's most extensive and ambitious application of RCI. The agreements will strengthen the rules-based trading system, heighten confidence in Asian and Pacific markets, and support a more vibrant trade and investment environment. Some signatories to the Regional Comprehensive Economic Partnership continue to encourage India to join the agreement to establish a dynamic South Asia–Southeast Asia–East Asia trade and investment network.

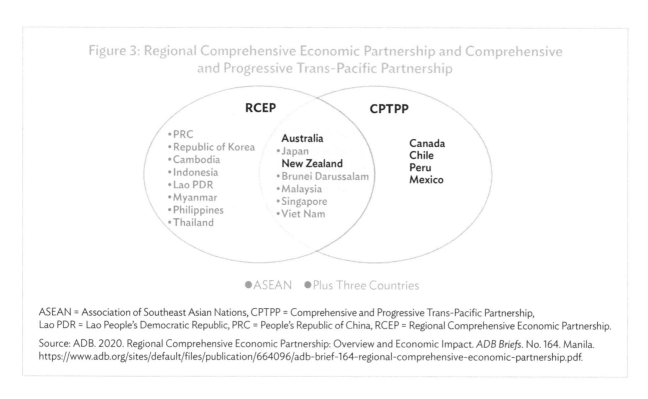

Figure 3: Regional Comprehensive Economic Partnership and Comprehensive and Progressive Trans-Pacific Partnership

ASEAN = Association of Southeast Asian Nations, CPTPP = Comprehensive and Progressive Trans-Pacific Partnership, Lao PDR = Lao People's Democratic Republic, PRC = People's Republic of China, RCEP = Regional Comprehensive Economic Partnership.

Source: ADB. 2020. Regional Comprehensive Economic Partnership: Overview and Economic Impact. *ADB Briefs*. No. 164. Manila. https://www.adb.org/sites/default/files/publication/664096/adb-brief-164-regional-comprehensive-economic-partnership.pdf.

Increasing cross-border risks, including climate change-related ones. About 70% of total global greenhouse gas (GHG) emissions arise from 10 countries, three of which are ADB developing member countries (DMCs), and almost half of global GHG emissions are from countries in Asia and the Pacific. The GHG emissions could increase further alongside economic growth, greater urbanization, changes in land use and consumption, possible expansion of fossil fuel-based energy production, and increased transport. The DMCs will be increasingly exposed and vulnerable to natural hazards and impacts of climate change, such as the growing frequency and intensity of extreme weather events, sea-level rise, changes in rainfall patterns, and increasing temperatures.[4] By 2030, parts of Asia may have average temperatures that lead to heightened risks for heat waves, extreme precipitation events, severe typhoons, drought, and changes in water supply.[5]

[4]   ADB. 2019. *Strategy 2030 Operational Plan for Priority 3: Tackling Climate Change, Building Climate and Disaster Resilience, and Enhancing Environmental Sustainability, 2019–2024.* Manila.

[5]   McKinsey Global Institute. 2020. *Climate Risk and Response in Asia,* https://www.mckinsey.com/business-functions/sustainability/our-insights/climate-risk-and-response-in-asia.

COVID-19's impacts on RCI in the Asia and Pacific region. *Trade fell, then rebounded* (Figure 4). Border closures, lockdowns, quarantines, and other means to control the virus disrupted the region's supply chains, putting at risk market access to emergency goods, and weakened demand for goods and services. Trade within Asia declined during the first half of 2020. Yet, increased demand for goods related to the COVID-19 pandemic and for electronics drove a rebound in developing Asia's exports. The bounce-back in exports resulted in only a modest 0.5% decline in the region's exports in 2020. Performance, however, varied across subregions. *Tourism imploded while remittances were broadly steady.* Tourism collapsed in all economies. In January–April 2020, international tourist arrivals fell to almost zero across most of the region and have yet to recover. Remittances declined in many economies as border closures halted market-based labor migration, but remittances increased in several other countries. *Investment declined significantly.* The COVID-19 pandemic accentuated the prevailing downward trend in greenfield foreign direct investment inflows. Greenfield outflows declined by almost half in 2020 compared with 2019. The value of announced intra-regional greenfield investments dropped by 45% for January–August 2020 compared with the same period in 2019.

Figure 4: Regional Cooperation and Integration-Related Impacts of COVID-19

50% decline in region exports

0% international tourist arrivals between Jan-Apr 2020

45% drop in intra-regional greenfield investments for Jan-Aug 2020*

Tourism imploded; remittances were broadly steady.

Significant declines in investment.

Trade fell, then rebounded.

- Border closures, lockdowns, quarantines, and other means to control the virus spread disrupted the region's supply chains.

- Intra-regional trade within Asia declined during the first half of 2020. Yet, increased demand for goods related to the COVID-19 pandemic and electronics drove a rebound in developing Asia's exports.

- Tourism collapsed in all economies.

- Remittances declined in many economies as border closures halted market-based labor migration, yet remittances increased in several other countries.

- The COVID-19 pandemic accentuated the prevailing downward trend in greenfield FDI inflows to the region.

COVID-19 = coronavirus disease, FDI = foreign direct investment.

*compared to the same period in 2019.

Source: ADB.

New cross-border needs and opportunities toward inclusive, resilient, and sustainable recovery. Collectively, countries are better aware of the need for more people-centered development, and they need to work together collaboratively and effectively through RCI initiatives.[6] The COVID-19-induced behavioral trends and expectations generated new demands and prospects. People want more secure cross-border private and public e-commerce and e-government services in education, health care, environmental management, and banking and finance, plus more accessible and reliable digital and information communication and technology platforms for digital trade and cross-border finance. The combination of the Asia and Pacific region's long-term rising economic strength, development and adoption of new digital technologies, changes in work and business and consumer spending caused by COVID-19, and increasing integration are creating cross-border demands that will become key components of post-COVID-19 recovery.

[6]   UNESCAP, ADB, and UNDP. 2021. *Responding to the COVID-19 Pandemic: Leaving No Country Behind.* Bangkok.

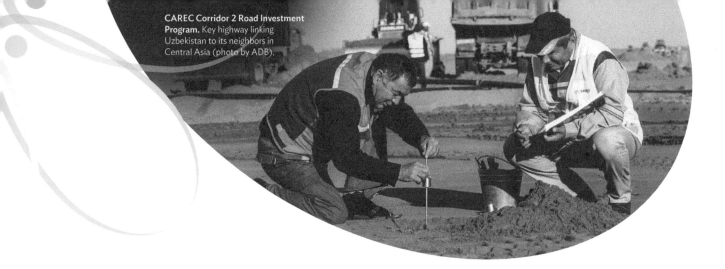

CAREC Corridor 2 Road Investment Program. Key highway linking Uzbekistan to its neighbors in Central Asia (photo by ADB).

III. EVOLUTION OF ADB'S REGIONAL COOPERATION AND INTEGRATION STRATEGIC AGENDA AND FRAMEWORK

ADB's Strategy 2030 and RCI operational plan. During the period of 2017–2020, ADB transitioned from its Long-Term Strategy 2020 (2008) and the Operational Plan for Regional Cooperation and Integration, 2016–2020 (November 2016) to Long-Term Strategy 2030 (July 2019) and Operational Plan 7: Fostering Regional Cooperation and Integration (OP7) (November 2019). The elements of the RCI strategic agenda set out in OP7 are causally linked (Figure 5). The three strategic operational pillars—connectivity, trade and investment, and regional public goods (RPGs)—and associated operational approaches, plus six implementation approaches, define OP7's strategic agenda and framework. The OP7 guides the formulation and execution of a coherent program of RCI operations supporting Strategy 2030, and uses a two-level results framework for each pillar (Figure 6). Results are monitored under ADB's corporate results framework and reported annually in ADB's Development Effectiveness Review.

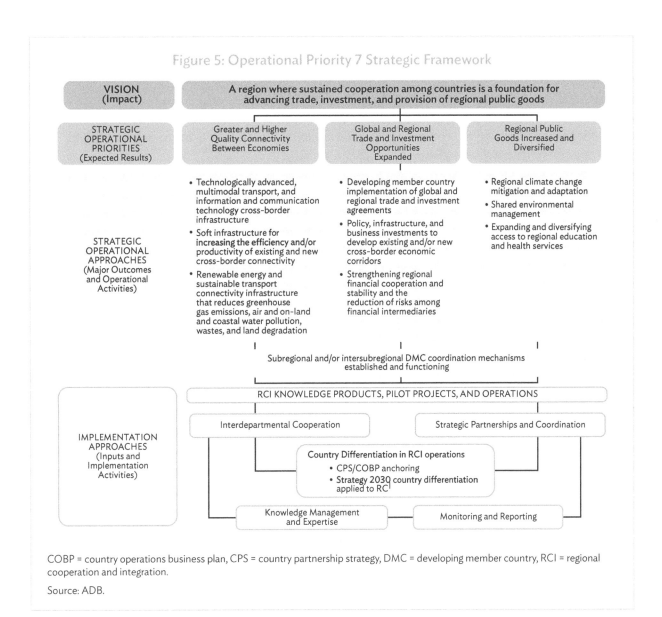

Figure 5: Operational Priority 7 Strategic Framework

COBP = country operations business plan, CPS = country partnership strategy, DMC = developing member country, RCI = regional cooperation and integration.

Source: ADB.

Figure 6: Regional Cooperation and Integration Results Framework
under Operational Priority 7

Pillar	Description	Indicator with Achievement Rate Target	Sub-pillars
1	Greater and higher quality connectivity between economies	**Cargo transported and energy transmitted across borders ($)**	Transport and ICT connectivity assets established or improved (number)
			Measures to improve the efficiency and/or productivity of cross-border connectivity supported in implementation (number)
			Clean energy capacity for power trade installed or improved (megawatt equivalent)
			Regional or subregional mechanisms created or operationalized to enhance coordination and cooperation among DMCs in energy, transport, or ICT connectivity (number)
2	Global and regional trade and investment opportunities expanded	**Trade and investment facilitated ($)**	Measures to improve execution of provisions in existing or new trade or investment agreements supported in implementation (number)
			Measures to develop existing and/or new cross-border economic corridors supported in implementation (number)
			Measures to improve regional financial cooperation supported in implementation (number)
			Regional or subregional mechanisms created or operationalized to enhance coordination and cooperation among DMCs in trade, finance, or multisector economic corridors (number)
3	Regional public goods increased and diversified	**Regional public goods initiatives successfully reducing cross-border environment or health risks, or providing regional access to education services (number)**	Measures to improve shared capacity of DMCs to mitigate or adapt to climate change supported in implementation (number)
			Measures to expand cross-border environmental protection and sustainable management of shared natural resources supported in implementation (number)
			Measures to improve regional public health and education services supported in implementation (number)
			Regional or subregional mechanisms created or operationalized to enhance coordination and cooperation among DMCs on regional public goods (number)

DMC = developing member country, ICT = information and communication technology.

Note: Indicators in bold font are results framework indicators; the rest are tracking indicators.

Source: ADB. 2019. ADB Corporate Results Framework, 2019-2024.

Giant cranes loading container vans into a ship at Danang Port. The Port is the third largest port system in Viet Nam and lies at the eastern end of the GMS East–West Economic Corridor (EWEC (photo by ADB).

IV. "ONE ADB" APPROACH AND ARCHITECTURE WITH THE REGIONAL COOPERATION AND INTEGRATION THEMATIC GROUP COMMUNITY

"One ADB." The RCI-TG community exemplifies the "One ADB" approach and organization architecture for implementing OP7. The "One ADB" RCI architecture maximizes all ADB's structures including the six operations departments (and their resident missions): the Office of Public–Private Partnerships (OPPP); the Sustainable Development and Climate Change Department (SDCC); the Regional Cooperation and Integration Division (ERCI), Economic Research and Regional Cooperation Department; the Budget, People, and Management Systems Department (BPMSD); the Strategy, Policy, and Partnerships Department (SPD); the Independent Evaluation Department (IED); and the ADB Institute. A schematic diagram of the "One ADB" approach to supporting DMCs through RCI initiatives is presented in Figure 7. The RCI operations are coordinated by the RCI-TG Committee, representing a broader RCI community.

RCI Community. The community is made up of the RCI-TG Committee; the RCI-TG Secretariat, which is in the SDCC; and 57 RCI experts in the operations departments[7] (Figure 8).[8] The community is guided by the committee, comprising the chief of the secretariat, six senior staff with RCI leadership responsibilities in each operations department, and a senior staff member of ERCI. The committee's principal responsibilities include (i) guiding the preparation and implementation of the secretariat's work plan, (ii) providing strategic guidance and economic analysis on new RCI thematic issues and trends that have operational relevance to ADB and on training needs and learning and development interventions, (iii) guiding the RCI project peer review exercise and prioritizing RCI knowledge products and thematic events, and (iv) reviewing and recommending approval of proposals for financing from trust funds. The committee meets at least once a quarter and often more frequently. The full committee engages with ADB Management, upon request.

....

[7]   Based on inputs (July 2021) from the operations departments on the staff members (international and national) working on RCI projects.
[8]   Central and West Asia, East Asia, Pacific, Private Sector Operations, South Asia, and Southeast Asia departments.

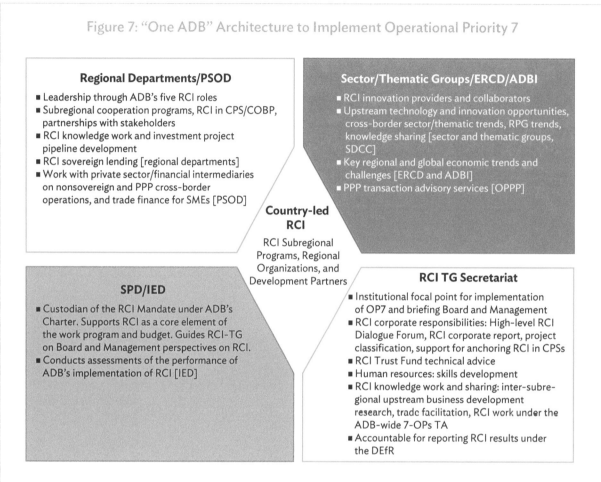

Figure 7: "One ADB" Architecture to Implement Operational Priority 7

Regional Departments/PSOD
- Leadership through ADB's five RCI roles
- Subregional cooperation programs, RCI in CPS/COBP, partnerships with stakeholders
- RCI knowledge work and investment project pipeline development
- RCI sovereign lending [regional departments]
- Work with private sector/financial intermediaries on nonsovereign and PPP cross-border operations, and trade finance for SMEs [PSOD]

Sector/Thematic Groups/ERCD/ADBI
- RCI innovation providers and collaborators
- Upstream technology and innovation opportunities, cross-border sector/thematic trends, RPG trends, knowledge sharing [sector and thematic groups, SDCC]
- Key regional and global economic trends and challenges [ERCD and ADBI]
- PPP transaction advisory services [OPPP]

Country-led RCI
RCI Subregional Programs, Regional Organizations, and Development Partners

SPD/IED
- Custodian of the RCI Mandate under ADB's Charter. Supports RCI as a core element of the work program and budget. Guides RCI-TG on Board and Management perspectives on RCI.
- Conducts assessments of the performance of ADB's implementation of RCI [IED]

RCI TG Secretariat
- Institutional focal point for implementation of OP7 and briefing Board and Management
- RCI corporate responsibilities: High-level RCI Dialogue Forum, RCI corporate report, project classification, support for anchoring RCI in CPSs
- RCI Trust Fund technical advice
- Human resources: skills development
- RCI knowledge work and sharing: inter-subregional upstream business development research, trade facilitation, RCI work under the ADB-wide 7-OPs TA
- Accountable for reporting RCI results under the DEfR

ADB = Asian Development Bank; ADBI = ADB Institute; CPS = country partnership strategy; COBP = country operations business plan; DEfR = development effectiveness review; ERCD = Economic Research and Regional Cooperation Department; IED = Independent Evaluation Department; OP7 = Operational Priority 7; OPPP = Office of Public–Private Partnership; PPP = public–private partnership; PSOD = Private Sector Operations Department; RCI-TG = Regional Cooperation and Integration Thematic Group; RPG = regional public good; SDCC = Sustainable Development and Climate Change Department; SMEs = small and medium-sized enterprises; SPD = Strategy, Policy, and Partnerships Department; TA = technical assistance.

Source: ADB.

The committee is supported on RCI matters by the RCI-TG acting as its secretariat. The secretariat's responsibilities are principally (i) supporting the committee's work program; (ii) leading resource mobilization from internal and external sources to finance RCI technical assistance (TA) operations; (iii) reviewing proposed RCI loan, grant, and TA operations; (iv) advising SPD on allocating RCI set-aside resources to specific operations; (iv) advising BPMSD on human resource planning to source and develop RCI skills and competencies in ADB; (v) undertaking specific knowledge operations to identify and pilot-test new and innovative lines of RCI investment operations; and (vi) organizing flagship RCI knowledge events, including the biennial RCI conference, and preparing a periodic RCI corporate report. The secretariat consults and collaborates closely with the other six Strategy 2030 operational priority and sector and thematic units in SDCC.

Figure 8: Regional Cooperation and Integration Thematic Group Community

CWRD = Central and West Asia Department; CWRC = Regional Cooperation and Operations Coordination Division, CWRD; EAPF = Public Management, Financial Sector, and Regional Cooperation Division, EARD; EARD = East Asia Department; ERCI = Regional Cooperation and Integration Division, Economic Research and Regional Cooperation Department; PARD = Pacific Department; OIC = officer-in-charge; PSOD = Private Sector Operations Department; RCI = regional cooperation and integration; SARC = Regional Cooperation and Operations Coordination Division, SARD; SARD = South Asia Department; SERC = Regional Cooperation and Operations Coordination Division, SERD; SERD = Southeast Asia Department.

Source: ADB.

Operations departments (five regional departments and PSOD), OPPP, and sector and thematic groups under the SDCC. ADB's operations departments execute RCI mainly through the Central Asia Regional Economic Cooperation (CAREC), the Greater Mekong Subregion (GMS), the South Asia Subregional Economic Cooperation (SASEC), and the Pacific Islands Forum,[9] and in cooperation with the other six Strategy 2030 operational priority groups plus sector units in SDCC that are recognized innovation providers and collaborators for upstream technology and innovation, cross-border sector/thematic trends, and knowledge sharing.[10] Each RCI subregional forum exercises convening power to bring together senior country officials to plan and implement an agreed subregional program framework. ADB offers impartial and professional knowledge services and, when requested, coordination and intermediation services to support intercountry economic cooperation, including—in the case of CAREC, GMS, and SASEC—secretariat services. The RCI units in the five regional departments, in cooperation with resident missions, continue to adjust the scope and balance of their resources to provide critical secretariat

---

9   The Pacific Islands Forum is an intra-government organization that aims to strengthen cooperation between countries and territories of the Pacific Ocean.

10 For example, the Urban Sector Group, through the Urban Climate Change Resilience Trust Fund, has piloted approaches relevant to cross-border climate change and resilience issues such as air pollution, disaster risk finance, integrated flood risk management, and use of earth observation technologies.

support, expedite RCI knowledge activities and policy dialogue to develop new RCI pipelines, conduct economic analyses supporting RCI project classification, prioritize projects for RCI set-aside financing, manage external RCI partnerships, and support in-country and intercountry coordination among national sector institutions for RCI project planning and implementation. On all aspects of RCI program management, the RCI units coordinate with their departments' sector divisions and resident missions, other regional departments, and the RCI-TG Secretariat. The Private Sector Operations Department (PSOD) supports nonsovereign investment in innovative, pioneering cross-border operations, and valuable and innovative trade finance. The OPPP provides transaction advisory services for public–private partnership cross-border operations.

ERCI, Economic Research and Regional Cooperation Department; and ADB Institute. ERCI promotes RCI as a strategic operational priority by (i) undertaking RCI-related research on the RCI pillars, (ii) providing operations support in line with the RCI operational plan, and (iii) supporting ADB participation in major regional and global policy forums. ERCI produces a regular annual flagship publication—the *Asian Economic Integration Report*—and periodic reports on RCI progress concerned with aid-for-trade, trade facilitation, macro-financial surveillance, and RCI progress in the ASEAN+3;[1] and other RCI-related thematic studies that are relevant to governments both in the current context and in the foreseeable future, such as regional connectivity, trade and investment, tourism, technology, supply chain, and RPGs. With its role of a gateway for collaboration with other international organization working on regional cooperation agendas, ERCI coordinates support for ADB and ADB Management participation in ASEAN and ASEAN+3, the Asia-Pacific Economic Community, the Asia–Europe Meeting, and other global and regional economic policy dialogues and forums that go beyond individual subregions. ERCI also works with the ASEAN+3 Macroeconomic Research Office, the United Nations Economic and Social Commission for Asia and the Pacific, and Asia Pacific think-tanks on different topics of cooperation to bring the best knowledge and capacity-building activities to interested stakeholders. The RCI-related knowledge work of the ADB Institute is a resource for understanding regional and global economic trends and challenges impacting RCI.

BPMSD, IED, and SPD. The BPMSD and the RCI-TG Secretariat cooperate on RCI-related workforce planning, skills development and deployment, training and career development, and recruitment. The IED assesses ADB's implementation of RCI. The SPD is the custodian of the RCI mandate under ADB's Charter, supporting RCI as a core element of the ADB's work program and budget, determining RCI set-aside resource allocation, and guiding the secretariat on ADB Board and Management perspectives on RCI.

Noi Bai-Lao Cai Highway. The highway decreased the cost of travel, which encouraged economic activities in the project area and employment opportunities for the local population, and improved access to social services (photo by ADB).

V. TRENDS IN ADB'S REGIONAL COOPERATION AND INTEGRATION LOANS, GRANTS, AND TECHNICAL ASSISTANCE, 2017–2020

This section discusses the main trends and features of ADB's RCI loans, grants, and TA of the six operations departments in 2017–2020.

Overview of Regional Cooperation and Integration Loans and Grants

Discontinued corporate target for RCI lending operations. In 2017–2019, under the previous 2016–2020 RCI Operational Plan, the share of ADB's RCI loan and grant operations remained below the then Strategy 2020 target of 30% of ADB's overall annual commitments (Figure 9). Under the Strategy 2030 and OP7, no similar target was set. However, with a large share in COVID-19 Pandemic Response Option (CPRO) operations in 2020, RCI significantly exceeded that legacy benchmark in volume but remained below it in number of projects, an indication that sizes of RCI projects were much larger in 2020.

Sector and regional balance. The transport sector continued to dominate the RCI portfolio in 2017–2020, otherwise considerable sector diversification was achieved; however, the exceedingly low share of sovereign and nonsovereign operations in ICT merits concerted attention. The high share of public sector management (PSM) operations reflects the large CPRO operations approved in 2020 that included important RCI dimensions (Section VI). Southeast Asia and Central West Asia were the major recipients of ADB's RCI operations, followed by South Asia, East Asia, and the Pacific.

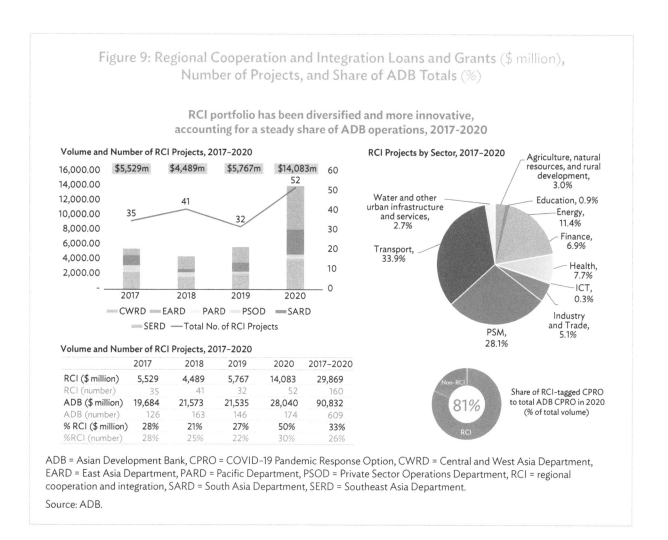

Figure 9: Regional Cooperation and Integration Loans and Grants ($ million), Number of Projects, and Share of ADB Totals (%)

RCI portfolio has been diversified and more innovative, accounting for a steady share of ADB operations, 2017-2020

Volume and Number of RCI Projects, 2017–2020

	2017	2018	2019	2020	2017–2020
RCI ($ million)	5,529	4,489	5,767	14,083	29,869
RCI (number)	35	41	32	52	160
ADB ($ million)	19,684	21,573	21,535	28,040	90,832
ADB (number)	126	163	146	174	609
% RCI ($ million)	28%	21%	27%	50%	33%
%RCI (number)	28%	25%	22%	30%	26%

ADB = Asian Development Bank, CPRO = COVID-19 Pandemic Response Option, CWRD = Central and West Asia Department, EARD = East Asia Department, PARD = Pacific Department, PSOD = Private Sector Operations Department, RCI = regional cooperation and integration, SARD = South Asia Department, SERD = Southeast Asia Department.

Source: ADB.

The share of nonsovereign RCI operations was notable by volume and number. This is presented in Figure 10, a result that should be reinforced and strengthened going forward, in line with the anticipated increase in private sector cross-border flows resulting from implementation of the Regional Comprehensive Economic Partnership, among other large trade agreements involving participation of the region's developing countries. Finance is one of the nascent sectors that is increasingly gaining visibility. Finance is the third most important sector where RCI nonsovereign lending was concentrated in the period 2017–2020, and there is certainly potential for a more digitized finance sector to operate within other sectors (e.g., agriculture value chains) across subregions.

The RCI loan and grant portfolio was generally balanced across RCI operational pillars, as presented in Figure 11. Sector diversification contributed to reasonably balanced implementation of activities across the RCI operational pillars, albeit with limited diversification into RPGs, a result that also merits concerted attention.

Some exemplary RCI loan and grant operations. Innovation was important in developing the RCI loan and grant portfolio in response to regional trends, such as greater adoption of digital technologies in many economic sectors, growth of digital trade, growth of agriculture-based value chains, and collective action among small economies to purchase in the international market competitively priced products with high economic and social benefits such as vaccines. ADB's RCI invested in applying innovative technologies using innovative approaches to achieve new or better development outcomes (Boxes 1, 2, and 3).

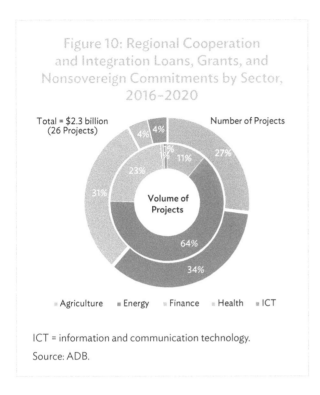

Figure 10: Regional Cooperation and Integration Loans, Grants, and Nonsovereign Commitments by Sector, 2016–2020

Total = $2.3 billion
(26 Projects)

Number of Projects

Volume of Projects

- Agriculture
- Energy
- Finance
- Health
- ICT

ICT = information and communication technology.

Source: ADB.

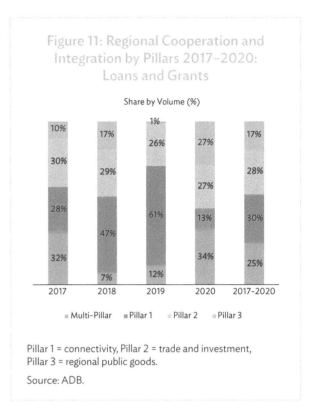

Figure 11: Regional Cooperation and Integration by Pillars 2017–2020: Loans and Grants

Share by Volume (%)

- Multi-Pillar
- Pillar 1
- Pillar 2
- Pillar 3

Pillar 1 = connectivity, Pillar 2 = trade and investment, Pillar 3 = regional public goods.

Source: ADB.

Box 1: Asia-Pacific Remote Broadband Internet Satellite Project: ADB's First Satellite Financing to Reach the Last Mile of Internet Access

Operational Priority 7, Pillar 1—Connectivity

More than 2 billion people in the Asia and Pacific region do not have reliable internet access because of inadequate infrastructure, geographical challenges, and the high cost of services. At the end of 2018, mobile internet penetration in the Pacific island countries was at just 18% of the population, the lowest in the world. To make broadband internet connections more widely available, the Asian Development Bank (ADB) launched its first satellite financing through the Asia-Pacific Remote Broadband Internet Satellite Project in 2019. The financing consists of a $25 million loan from ADB and a $25 million ADB-administered loan from the Leading Asia's Private Infrastructure Fund to Kacific Broadband Satellites International Limited. Leading Asia's Private Infrastructure

Kacific1 as it orbits Asia and the Pacific (artist's impression) (photo by Kacific/SpaceX).

Fund is an ADB vehicle for cofinancing private sector infrastructure. ADB works with GuarantCo to guarantee additional private cofinancing for the project. ADB's participation has helped leverage the financing for the highly developmental project. It supports the construction, launch, and operation of Kacific-1, a shared geostationary earth orbit, high-throughput satellite. Equipped with Ka-band technology, Kacific-1 will deliver the most powerful signal ever achieved by a commercial satellite in the region. Kacific-1 will provide affordable high-speed broadband internet access to remote and rural communities that are typically beyond the reach of traditional fiber optics. ADB sees these innovative technologies as vital for bringing inclusive development to unserved and underserved areas through improved access to information, better education and health services, and greater connectivity and trade among countries.

Source: ADB. 2019. *Reports and Recommendations of the President: Asia-Pacific Remote Broadband Internet Satellite.* Manila. https://www.adb.org/projects/documents/reg-53115-001-rrp.

Box 2: Greater Mekong Subregion Climate-Friendly Agribusiness Value Chain:
Climate-Friendly and Innovative Solutions to Boost Agribusiness

Operational Priority 7, Pillar 2—Trade and Investment

Agriculture comprises a sizeable chunk of the Greater Mekong Subregion economies but consists mainly of subsistence farming. Agribusiness value chains remain fragmented and underdeveloped because of insufficient infrastructure, weak policy environment for agribusiness, and lack of climate mitigation and adaptation efforts to deal with vulnerability to floods and drought. The Greater Mekong Subregion Climate-Friendly Agribusiness Value Chain project, approved in 2018, aims to strengthen climate resilience and to modernize agriculture using advanced technologies in Cambodia, the Lao People's Democratic Republic (Lao PDR), and Myanmar. Through the project, the Asian Development Bank (ADB) will strengthen the capacity of farmers and agribusiness for climate-smart agriculture. To promote sustainability along the value chain, the project will help create a favorable agribusiness environment, including climate-friendly agribusiness policies and standards, green finance and risk-sharing mechanisms, and climate risk management through information and communication technology.

Source: ADB.

Box 3: Systems Strengthening for Effective Coverage of New Vaccines in the Pacific:
Pooled Procurement for Equitable Access to Life-Saving Vaccines

Operational Priority 7, Pillar 3—Regional Public Goods

Cervical cancer is the second-leading cause of death for women in the Pacific, next to heart disease and stroke. Roughly 70% of such cancer cases are caused by the sexually transmitted human papillomavirus (HPV) and are largely preventable through early detection and HPV vaccination. However, screening programs and awareness in most Pacific countries are wanting. Two other easily preventable diseases—pneumonia and diarrhea—are liable for three in 10 deaths of children under the age of 5 in Pacific island countries.

The Systems Strengthening for Effective Coverage of New Vaccines in the Pacific Project, approved in 2018, adopts a regional approach to reduce the number of cervical cancer cases and other infectious diseases in children and women in Samoa, Tonga, Tuvalu, and Vanuatu. The Asian Development Bank (ADB) committed $25 million to finance the pooled procurement of HPV, rotavirus, and pneumococcus conjugate vaccines though the United Nations Children's Fund (UNICEF) global medical procurement scheme. Pooled procurement allows the small countries to take advantage of lower prices, quality products, and technical expertise in vaccines and cold chain management as well as emergency stockpiles that would otherwise not be accessible to them. The project finance design includes phased cofinancing of vaccines with countries to promote effective budget absorption of costs. Country ownership is crucial in providing effective immunization services and affordable quality vaccines. More than 580,000 people across the four countries are expected to benefit from more efficient primary health services because of the project.

The System Strengthening for Effective Coverage of New Vaccines in the Pacific Project is supporting the health ministries in immunizing 90,700 children against pneumonia, 71,600 children against rotavirus, and 84,200 adolescent girls against HPV infections in Samoa, Tonga, Tuvalu, and Vanuatu (photo by ADB).

Source: ADB.

The RCI portfolio in 2021 remains above pre-pandemic levels, continues to diversify, and the SARD grouping of DMCs may receive the largest allocation. In 2021, the RCI portfolio is expected to remain above pre-pandemic levels in terms of volume of commitments and number of operations; to exhibit good sector diversification (albeit, again minimal investment into ICT) particularly a large expansion into the health sector; maintain a sizable participation in CPRO operations; and approaches the pre-Strategy 2030 target of 30% (by volume) of total ADB annual commitments. The grouping of DMCs assisted by ADB's SARD is projected to account for approximately 50% of the volume of RCI assistance in 2021 (Figure 12).[11]

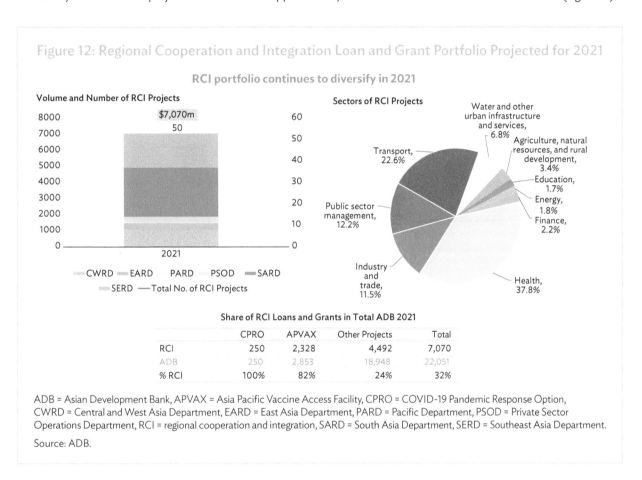

Figure 12: Regional Cooperation and Integration Loan and Grant Portfolio Projected for 2021

RCI portfolio continues to diversify in 2021

Share of RCI Loans and Grants in Total ADB 2021

	CPRO	APVAX	Other Projects	Total
RCI	250	2,328	4,492	7,070
ADB	250	2,853	18,948	22,051
% RCI	100%	82%	24%	32%

ADB = Asian Development Bank, APVAX = Asia Pacific Vaccine Access Facility, CPRO = COVID-19 Pandemic Response Option, CWRD = Central and West Asia Department, EARD = East Asia Department, PARD = Pacific Department, PSOD = Private Sector Operations Department, RCI = regional cooperation and integration, SARD = South Asia Department, SERD = Southeast Asia Department.

Source: ADB.

Overview of Technical Assistance for Regional Cooperation and Integration

The RCI TA portfolio registered an upward trend. The six operations departments' RCI TA grew robustly in 2017–2019, with South Asia at the forefront. Overall, however, TA operations were well balanced across the subregions, including a sizable allocation to the Pacific. Growth declined moderately in 2020 (Figure 13).

The RCI TA portfolio was generally well diversified among sectors and themes (Figure 14), reflecting the need for concerted upstream knowledge and capacity-building services before DMCs and ADB agreed to commit to a new sector or subsector with longer-term potential for future loan and grant pipeline development.

[11]   The information presented in Figure 12 is indicative only and may be subject to change by the end of 2021.

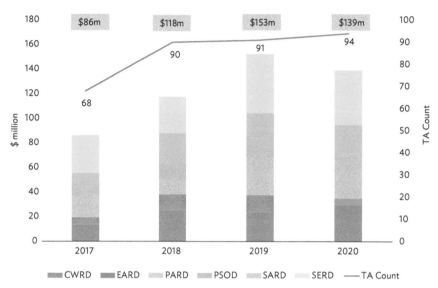

Figure 13: Regional Cooperation and Integration Portfolio 2017–2020: Technical Assistance (volume, number)

CWRD = Central and West Asia Department, EARD = East Asia Department, PARD = Pacific Department, PSOD = Private Sector Operations Department, SARD = South Asia Department, SERD = Southeast Asia Department, TA = technical assistance.

Source: ADB.

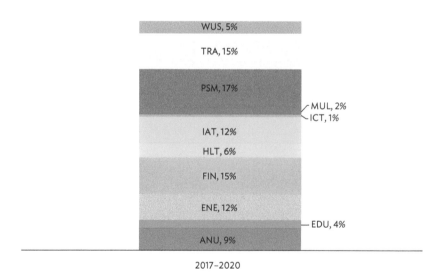

Figure 14: Regional Cooperation and Integration Technical Assistance: Projects by Sector, 2017–2020

ANU = agriculture and natural resources, EDU = education, ENE = energy, FIN = finance, HLT = health, IAT = industry and trade, ICT = information and communication technology, MUL=multisector, PSM = public sector management, TRA = transport, WUS = water and other urban infrastructure and services.

Source: ADB.

Modality-wise, knowledge and support TA represented 72% of the operations departments' combined RCI TA in 2017–2020 (Figure 15). This is expected, considering the nature of RCI TA operations in providing institutional, advisory, and capacity-building support, in addition to project preparation for RCI-relevant investment.

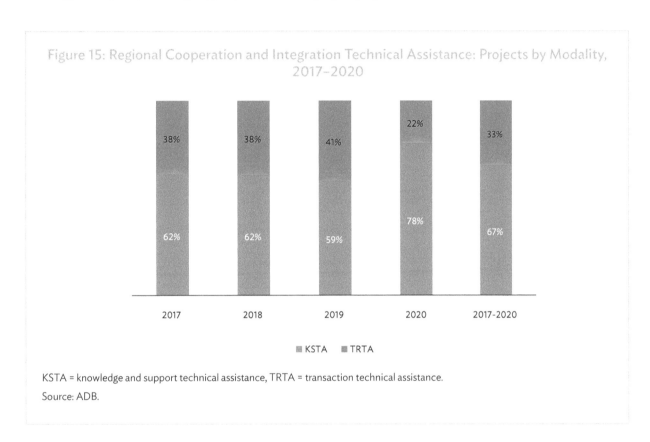

Figure 15: Regional Cooperation and Integration Technical Assistance: Projects by Modality, 2017–2020

KSTA = knowledge and support technical assistance, TRTA = transaction technical assistance.
Source: ADB.

Some exemplary RCI TA operations. The RCI TA focused on innovation under each RCI operational pillar: for example, applying innovative technologies and associated management practices, promoting new areas for cross-border collective action, and pilot-testing innovative development-finance mechanisms to deliver greater RPGs. The innovative TA operations in Boxes 4, 5, and 6 could expand inter-subregional RCI, reducing the costs of trade for landlocked countries, and make disaster risk management significantly more affordable and cost-effective. If the TA projects are successful, their outputs can be shared with other DMCs and potentially replicated across the Asia and Pacific region.

Box 4: Advancing Maritime Cooperation under the South Asia Subregional Economic Cooperation: Cooperation is Key for the Maritime Industry

Operational Priority 7, Pillar 1—Connectivity

Intra-regional trade and trade outside South Asia—mostly maritime—are expected to continue to increase significantly. The importance of maritime connectivity has been highlighted since Maldives and Sri Lanka joined the South Asia Subregional Economic Cooperation (SASEC) in 2014, and Myanmar joined in 2017. Yet, SASEC does not have a modal cooperation mechanism for maritime transport. Maritime connectivity among SASEC member countries is limited by various factors, including the high cost of trade and transport, manual data exchange between parties in the port community, prolonged cargo clearance procedures, limited inland transport and port infrastructure, legal and regulatory barriers, and limited knowledge of maritime cooperation and coordination and international best practices in port operations.

In 2019, the Asian Development Bank (ADB) provided $1.5 million for the Advancing Cooperation in the Maritime Sector in SASEC Program to integrate ports in five countries (Bangladesh, India, Maldives, Myanmar, and Sri Lanka) by leveraging advanced technologies, improving logistics infrastructure, promoting a sound regulatory environment, and building human resources and institutional capacity. The technical assistance supported analytical studies to identify a pipeline of maritime projects and initiatives to strengthen maritime connectivity and cooperation in South Asia: (i) port community system development plans, (ii) additional logistics infrastructure, (iii) cruise tourism, and (iv) greening strategies to promote healthy oceans through efficient pollution control and sustainable port infrastructure. The technical assistance supported effective dialogue, knowledge sharing, and capacity development of government agencies to resolve SASEC maritime issues, such as data-sharing limitations, legal and regulatory barriers, gaps in logistics infrastructure, and insufficient greening programs in port operations.

Source: ADB.

Box 5: Better Customs for Better Client Services in Central Asia Regional Economic Cooperation Countries: Using High-Level Technology in Customs Cooperation

Operational Priority 7, Pillar 2—Trade and Investment

Central Asia Regional Economic Cooperation (CAREC) customs agencies are crucial in encouraging trade, boosting competitiveness, and ensuring the smooth flow of goods and people across borders. However, slow adoption of modern technology solutions and weak national and cross-border coordination make the agencies ill-equipped to handle the increasingly complex trading rules and rising trade volume driven by e-commerce expansion.

The $1.4 million knowledge and support technical assistance, Better Customs for Better Client Services in CAREC Countries, approved in 2019, will help expand trade among CAREC countries by modernizing national trade facilitation environments and strengthening institutions. The technical assistance will promote digital customs technologies such as e-customs systems and paperless trade. The technical assistance will support the development and pilot implementation of the comprehensive, risk-based CAREC Advanced Transit System, which is supported by a custom-built information common exchange information technology system with the capacity to link into the European Union's New Computerized Transit System. High-level technology will be used to prepare inter-subregional transit trade agreements to strengthen supply chain security, help trade flow smoothly, and reduce costs.

The technical assistance will be instrumental in implementing the CAREC Integrated Trade Agenda 2030 by building the capacity of customs agencies and the CAREC Customs Cooperation Committee in logistics management and coordinated border management. The technical assistance will strengthen intra-regional trade among CAREC countries by building customs-to-customs cooperation and strengthening public–private sector dialogue and cooperation.

Source: Asian Development Bank.

Box 6: Developing a Disaster Risk Transfer Facility in the Central Asia Regional Economic Cooperation: Innovative Cross-Border Financing Mechanism for Disaster Risk Management

Operational Priority 7, Pillar 3—Regional Public Goods

The estimated economic losses from disasters in Central Asia Regional Economic Cooperation (CAREC) countries surpassed $22 billion in 2008–2018 and are expected to rise further as disasters become more frequent and intense with climate change. The CAREC countries have yet to fully develop and implement comprehensive disaster risk management strategies that can efficiently fill the protection gap. The capacity to integrate disaster risk reduction measures into development planning and budgeting processes is still inadequate. The development of, access to, and use of ex-ante disaster risk financing instruments for post-disaster response are still in their infancy in the CAREC countries. Given these constraints, the Asian Development Bank (ADB) approved in 2019 the $2.0 million knowledge and support technical assistance, Developing a Disaster Risk Transfer Facility in the CAREC Region, to support collaboration among CAREC countries in disaster risk financing. The technical assistance will (i) produce disaster risk assessments and state-of-the-art modeling to help governments make informed disaster risk management decisions and (ii) design a sustainable regional disaster risk transfer pilot scheme to manage disaster risk for selected CAREC countries. Regional and national workshops and knowledge-sharing events will be organized to help generate interest in and ownership of a regional disaster risk transfer facility in the CAREC region. A regional mechanism is effective in promoting stability among countries.

Source: ADB.

Establishing innovative RCI collective action mechanisms to address specialized sector/thematic challenges. The Economic Research and Regional Cooperation Department and SDCC—as well as some specialized domain units at ADB like the SPD—plan, support, and implement TA/grant-financed initiatives under ADB's corporate priorities that build innovative collective action among countries. These initiatives form partnerships among important stakeholders (individuals and organizations) from across many DMCs, to sustain dialogue and cooperation on the advancement of knowledge, institutional capabilities, and policy reforms to address important sector/thematic issues. These initiatives assist individual countries responding to their challenges through increased and more effective participation in regional and global economies and contribution to advancing regional and global public goods (see Boxes 7, 8, and 9).

Box 7: Knowledge and Support Technical Assistance: Strengthening Regional Cooperation and Integration Knowledge Partnerships and Research Network in Asia and the Pacific

This knowledge and support technical assistance (2018) strengthens knowledge partnerships on emerging sector/thematic themes (e.g., technology, labor mobility, and disaster risk reduction) relevant to regional cooperation and integration (RCI) by fostering and supporting research collaboration among policy research institutions in Asia and the Pacific. Cross-border collaboration needs to go beyond country-specific analysis of a common topic, to provide regional solutions and recommendations on the regional agenda. The resulting policy-relevant studies benefit developing member countries, policy makers, and ADB's regional departments, as they are designed for regional solutions to cross-border issues.

The knowledge and support technical assistance helps RCI practitioners overcome three constraints to collaborative RCI research. First, single-country RCI knowledge work may be scaled back if other countries share the benefits but not the costs. Second, joint research usually depends on preexisting relationships and partnerships. Third, the technical capacity of research institutions in the region varies substantially, with some such institutions lacking the resources to conduct joint RCI research.

continued on next page

Box 7 *continued*

The Asian Development Bank (ADB)-Asian Think Tanks Network (ATTN) is an informal group of think tanks actively engaged in research on sustainable growth and inclusive development in the Asia and Pacific region, supported in part by this knowledge and support technical assistance. The ATTN consists of over 40 member organizations based in ADB member countries, with strong representation of state economic development policy research institutions. The network aims to (i) enhance systematic knowledge sharing among member think tanks, specifically on development experiences and policy lessons, (ii) strengthen each think tank's capacity to generate knowledge or provide policy advice on its domain, and (iii) raise the region's voice in the international arena on issues related to economic growth and inclusive development.

The annual ATTN Forum serves as a platform for members to exchange views, discuss research work, and share experiences on pressing development concerns. Forums have been held on dedicated topics such as (i) innovation and inclusion, (ii) financing sustainable urbanization, and (iii) technology and human capital development. For example, the 2017 knowledge-sharing event held on 20–21 September 2017 in Colombo, Sri Lanka (attended by over 70 representatives from 25 countries in Asia and the Pacific and seven international organizations) presented research papers on the themes of public–private partnership and other innovative and emerging infrastructure financing schemes, and urban infrastructure and service delivery. Participants shared experiences, challenges, models, and opportunities for urban infrastructure projects, and their financing options. Discussions followed, complemented by lectures and presentations highlighting the fiscal implications of urbanization and the region's growing infrastructure needs. ADB serves as the ATTN's organizer and secretariat.

Source: Asian Development Bank. 2018. *Technical Assistance to Strengthening Regional Cooperation and Integration Knowledge Partnerships and Research Network in Asia and the Pacific.* Manila. https://www.adb.org/sites/default/files/project-documents/51291/51291-001-tar-en.pdf; ADB-Asian Think Tanks Network. https://asianthinktanks.adb.org/.

Box 8: Asia Pacific Tax Hub

With a charter mandate to foster economic growth, cooperation, and development, the Asian Development Bank (ADB) has recognized the importance of assisting its developing member countries to mitigate tax evasion and the attrition of their domestic tax bases. Over the period 2016–2020, ADB designed and implemented several technical assistance (TA) operations to increase the capacity and *regional cooperation of tax authorities* to widen and shield their domestic tax base, augment the capacity of tax administrations, improve domestic tax compliance, and develop better tools and procedures to restrict both cross-border and national tax evasion and avoidance. During the same period, these TAs were complemented by updating existing ADB policy as well as introducing new policy in relation to tax integrity, tax transparency, and establishing a trust fund to strengthen domestic resource mobilization.

At its 53rd Annual Meeting (September 2020), ADB announced the establishment of a regional hub for domestic resource mobilization and international tax cooperation (which was officially launched at ADB's 54th Annual Meeting, May 2021). The regional hub operates multiple functions such as institutional and capacity development, including sharing of information; knowledge dissemination among partners, international and bilateral financial and revenue organizations, and developing countries; and sustained close engagement across development stakeholders. The regional hub builds links among practitioners from tax policy entities as well as tax administration bodies of developing economies to advance needed progress in tax reform. In establishing the hub, ADB also mainstreams domestic resource mobilization and international tax cooperation in its operations such as TA and policy-based lending to assist governments strengthen their capacity for domestic resource mobilization and adoption of international tax standards.

Source: ADB. Asia Pacific Tax Hub. https://www.adb.org/what-we-do/asia-pacific-tax-hub.

Box 9: Continued Support for ASEAN+3 Asian Bond Markets Initiative

The Asian Development Bank (ADB) continued to support the ASEAN+3 Asian Bond Markets Initiative (ABMI) since its launch in 2002 by serving as its secretariat to provide technical support for the implementation of the initiative, most recently guided by the ASEAN+3 ABMI Medium-Term Road Map 2019–2022, endorsed by the ASEAN+3 Finance Ministers and Central Bank Governors in May 2019. Through ABMI collaboration, ASEAN+3 members continue to develop local currency (LCY) bond markets as an alternative source of funding to foreign currency-denominated bank loans to minimize the currency and maturity mismatches that had made the region vulnerable to the sudden reversal of capital inflows. The more developed and integrated LCY bond markets enabled economies in the region to mobilize domestic savings to fund long-term investment needs and mitigate their vulnerabilities to capital flow reversals.

Some key undertakings and support by ADB to the ABMI's four task forces during 2017–2020 are as follows:

1. **Promote the issuance of LCY-denominated bonds (Task Force 1 co-chaired by the People's Republic of China and Thailand):** In 2021, established a regional program to support corporate bond issuers in bringing green, social, and sustainability bonds to the market, including assistance on capacity building, transactions, and verification. Enhanced information dissemination of green bond market developments by creating a webpage in 2020 that included detailed guidance on the green bond issuance process, data, publications, and other relevant regional initiatives.

2. **Facilitate demand for LCY-denominated bonds (Task Force 2 co-chaired by Japan and Singapore):** Upgraded the AsianBondsOnline in 2018 from primarily a market data portal to a comprehensive information platform for ASEAN+3 bond markets. Revamped website to host two webpages jointly with Task Forces 1 and 3, and a Tracking Asia webpage to monitor macroeconomic information for stakeholders. Published the quarterly Asia Bond Monitor and innovated infographic newsletters, such as Weekly Debt Highlights, Monthly Debt Roundup, and ASEAN+3 Sustainable Bonds Highlights to track regional financial conditions, macroeconomic performance, and bond market development.

3. **Strengthen the regulatory framework (Task Force 3 co-chaired by Japan and Malaysia):** Provided secretariat function to the ASEAN+3 Bond Market Forum through the completion of the Bond Market Guides for 14 ASEAN+3 markets including Hong Kong, China, and the establishment of an ASEAN+3 Bond Market Forum webpage in 2021. Supported the creation of professional investors-only bond market in each market to expand the ASEAN+3 Multi-Currency Bond Issuance Framework, a common regional bond issuance program to standardize different bond issuance procedures. Currently, seven out of 14 markets in ASEAN+3 have adopted the ASEAN+3 Multi-Currency Bond Issuance Framework, while 12 bonds have been issued in five markets, including the first LCY corporate bond issued in Cambodia. Promoted the development of standards and regional frameworks in cross-border financial transaction reporting.

4. **Improve bond market infrastructure (Task Force 4 co-chaired by the Republic of Korea and the Philippines):** Provided secretariat role to the Cross-Border Settlement Infrastructure Forum to create an efficient regional settlement intermediary linking key market settlement infrastructures in the region. Produced relevant publications to raise awareness on the importance of regional market infrastructure for boosting intra-regional investments, the latest of which is a report published in 2020 on the progress toward the establishment of a regional settlement intermediary. Led the discussions during Cross-Border Settlement Infrastructure Forum meetings in reviewing the type of settlement infrastructure that would be best for the region amid the rapid technological changes.

The coronavirus disease (COVID-19) pandemic resulted in a sharp increase in public debts in developing member countries. To ensure smooth recovery from the pandemic, sustainable debt finance, especially through the LCY bond market, will play a more critical role. ADB will share the lessons from the ABMI to help developing member countries to develop their bond markets.

Source: AsianBondsOnline. https://asianbondsonline.adb.org/.

Kolkata Environmental Improvement Investment Program. Children play and fetch water from the the community tap at the Behala slum area in Kolkata, India (photo by ADB).

VI. INCORPORATING REGIONAL COOPERATION AND INTEGRATION IN MITIGATING THE COVID-19 PANDEMIC ACROSS ASIA AND THE PACIFIC

The COVID-19 pandemic has "left no country behind" in its wake across Asia and the Pacific. The pandemic worsened the quality of life in every DMC of ADB. The sudden onset and rapid spread of the pandemic spurred countries across the region to coordinate and cooperate closely with each other. ADB's COVID-19 response to support DMCs consists of a $20 billion package for the COVID-19 Pandemic Response Option (CPRO) announced in April 2020, and the $9 billion Asia Pacific Vaccine Access Facility (APVAX) announced in December 2020. ADB's initial $20 billion COVID-19 response package focuses on measures countering the severe macroeconomic and health impacts caused by COVID-19, while its $9 billion APVAX initiative offers rapid and equitable access through procuring and delivering effective and safe COVID-19 vaccines. The remainder of this chapter explains how ADB's RCI activities quickly and effectively supported DMCs' concerted efforts.

Incorporating RCI in CPRO operations. The RCI-TG helped (i) formulate the ADB-assisted CPRO-funded programs fostering specific types of joint action among DMC authorities to combat the pandemic and (ii) guide the allocation of some of the programs' resources to support small and medium-sized enterprises (SMEs) and employees working in the tradable sector. Adopting the RCI scorecard developed for Operational Priority 7 (OP7), operations departments and the RCI-TG Secretariat provided a staff guidance note to all CPRO-processing departments to help identify opportunities related to the following:

(i) improving private and public sector production and distribution, including through regional procurement of medical and/or food supplies and reduced tariffs and/or facilitated trade of priority supplies;

(ii) supporting key trade sectors to ensure resilience;

(iii)   ensuring that national responses to deal with COVID-19 are consistent with inter-DMC agreements or other commitments to implement joint surveillance measures or protocols on communicable diseases, guided by learning from other countries;

(iv)   reducing shared health risks; and

(v)   applying World Health Organization (WHO) standards to cross-border health protocols.

Where relevant, links are established to ADB regional TA ongoing or under preparation that could support or complement RCI components of the CPRO-assisted emergency program to further strengthen the coordinated regional health response. The RCI scorecard methodology provided a rational, structured approach to reviewing projects and aligning them with funding objectives and proved to be effective in helping direct targeted COVID-19 responses in RCI programs.

Two-thirds of CPRO projects referenced regional agreements on health and/or United Nations General Assembly Resolutions on solidarity and common action against COVID-19. Of CPRO projects, 75% supported one or more of the following: reduction in shared health risks (e.g., Azerbaijan, Kazakhstan, and Thailand); regional procurement of medical or food supplies (e.g., Solomon Islands and Cook Islands); and key trade sectors, SMEs and small-scale traders, and employment and livelihoods (e.g., Kyrgyz Republic, Mongolia, and Thailand). Two-thirds of CPRO projects supported one or more of the following: raising capacity of health systems to WHO standards (e.g., Kazakhstan and Kyrgyz Republic), undertaking regional information sharing and surveillance on health (e.g., Thailand), and building up regional emergency funds and equipment pools (Figure 16).

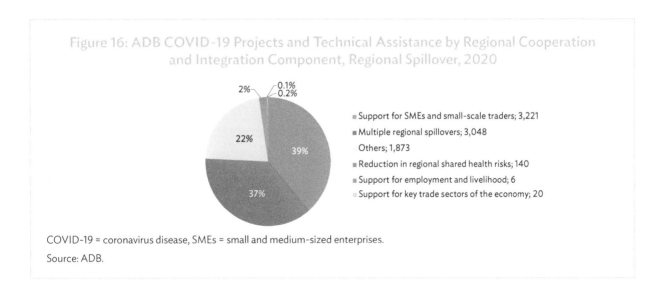

Figure 16: ADB COVID-19 Projects and Technical Assistance by Regional Cooperation and Integration Component, Regional Spillover, 2020

- Support for SMEs and small-scale traders; 3,221
- Multiple regional spillovers; 3,048
- Others; 1,873
- Reduction in regional shared health risks; 140
- Support for employment and livelihood; 6
- Support for key trade sectors of the economy; 20

COVID-19 = coronavirus disease, SMEs = small and medium-sized enterprises.
Source: ADB.

RCI COVID-19 emergency response TA. Regional Support to Address the Outbreak of Coronavirus Disease 2019 and Potential Outbreaks of Other Communicable Diseases[12] supported (i) short-term health security capacity building in individual DMCs; (ii) scaling up of regional approaches, including developing and disseminating regional risk communication materials to develop clear and accurate messaging and assuage public fears and uncertainty about the COVID-19 pandemic; and (iii) establishment of a multisector regional coordinating mechanism to procure

[12]   ADB. 2020. *Regional Support to Address the Outbreak of Coronavirus Disease 2019 and Potential Outbreaks of Other Communicable Diseases.* Manila.

and distribute medical supplies and to conduct disease surveillance and reporting. ADB convened discussions with the WHO Western Pacific Regional Office and the South-East Asia Regional Office, the International Monetary Fund, the World Bank, travel and airline associations, research institutions, and private sector communications firms. Mechanisms for routine discussions and consultations with several of the organizations have been formalized.

COVID-19 and the RCI Policy Open Dialogue Webinar Series[13] **and Asian Economic Integration Report 2021.** Throughout 2020, the RCI-TG and the Regional Cooperation and Integration Division, ERCI have been cooperating on the RCI Policy Open Dialogue webinars to discuss the nature and implications or impacts of and potential solutions to COVID-19-related issues in the emergency and recovery phases. Topics have included COVID-19's impact on trade and SMEs, tourism recovery and transformation, regional financial safety nets, regional supply chains, digitizing trade facilitation, and RCI and regionalization in the post-COVID-19 era (Figure 17). Participation by ADB and external experts and questions or other interventions from stakeholders contribute to better understanding of an issue and generate wider perspectives on approaches to resolve it through policy dialogue with DMCs, ADB knowledge products and services, and investment operations. Webinars build up the COVID-19-related knowledge base of ADB and other multilateral development banks in the region, which will be presented in a joint multilateral development bank report in late 2021. ADB's *Asian Economic Integration Report 2021* focused on how the pandemic impacted the Asia and Pacific region's global and regional trade and investment in 2020. The report analyzed high-frequency data and the associated potential of financial market risks and how the pandemic affected regional and country remittances and tourism receipts. Given the enormous opportunities a digital economy offers, particularly during the pandemic, and the problems associated with the widening digital divide, the report shed light on the economic potential that digitization can unlock and policy options to bridge the digital divide during the post-COVID-19 recovery.

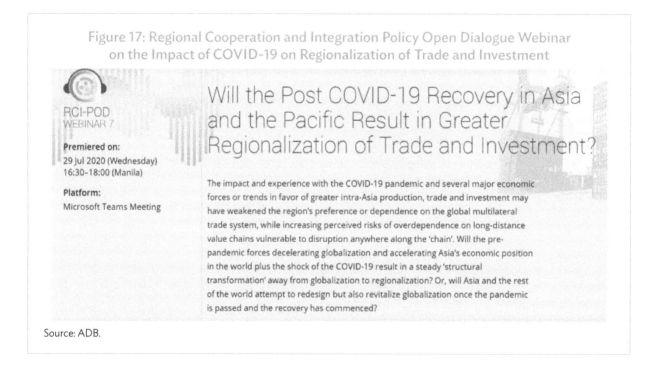

Figure 17: Regional Cooperation and Integration Policy Open Dialogue Webinar on the Impact of COVID-19 on Regionalization of Trade and Investment

RCI-POD
WEBINAR 7

Premiered on:
29 Jul 2020 (Wednesday)
16:30–18:00 (Manila)

Platform:
Microsoft Teams Meeting

Will the Post COVID-19 Recovery in Asia and the Pacific Result in Greater Regionalization of Trade and Investment?

The impact and experience with the COVID-19 pandemic and several major economic forces or trends in favor of greater intra-Asia production, trade and investment may have weakened the region's preference or dependence on the global multilateral trade system, while increasing perceived risks of overdependence on long-distance value chains vulnerable to disruption anywhere along the 'chain'. Will the pre-pandemic forces decelerating globalization and accelerating Asia's economic position in the world plus the shock of the COVID-19 result in a steady 'structural transformation' away from globalization to regionalization? Or, will Asia and the rest of the world attempt to redesign but also revitalize globalization once the pandemic is passed and the recovery has commenced?

Source: ADB.

---

[13] The webinar series is organized by ERCI and the RCI-TG to provide a venue for informal and open policy dialogue on RCI.

Leveraging RCI impact of APVAX operations. ADB is contributing significantly to vaccination across the region with the launch of its $9 billion APVAX initiative, offering rapid and equitable support to DMCs as they procure and deliver effective and safe COVID-19 vaccines. The COVID-19 vaccination programs reduce virus transmission within and between countries, which is essential to protect lives and achieve high-quality regional public health, while enabling people to safely work, travel, and engage in social activity in their countries and across borders. Various APVAX operations include diverse RCI benefits in pooled procurement of vaccines (e.g., Bangladesh, Georgia, Indonesia, Mongolia, and Samoa/Tonga/Tuvalu/Vanuatu under Systems Strengthening for Effective Coverage of New Vaccines in the Pacific); international logistics and related services (e.g., Afghanistan[14] and Tajikistan); cross-border tracking of vaccines (Bangladesh); sharing of regional surveillance and deployment information and knowledge (e.g., Indonesia, Nepal, the Philippines, and Sri Lanka); and coordinated approaches to border economic zones (Nepal). Table 1 shows the links between RCI elements of APVAX operations and regional benefits and outcomes.

Table 1: Regional Cooperation and Integration in ADB's Asia Pacific Vaccine Access Facility Operations

Projects	RCI-Related Components	Regional Economic Benefits	Additional Support to RCI
Afghanistan[a] COVID-19 Vaccine Support Project under the Asia Pacific Vaccine Access Facility	• The project supports (i) procurement of vaccines through COVAX; (ii) international and national logistics and related services; and (iii) capacity building in coordination with ongoing CAREC TA.	• Given Afghanistan's location at the crossroads of Central Asia, the project will generate significant regional public goods and complement efforts to contain the COVID-19 pandemic and foster growth in the CAREC region, through addressing pandemic risks and cross-border health threats.	• Additional benefits include addressing remaining poverty and reducing inequality and accelerating progress in gender equality. Strong partnerships with WHO ensures that support will enable Afghanistan to meet international guidelines and protocols.
Bangladesh Responsive COVID-19 Vaccines for Recovery Project Under the Asia Pacific Vaccine Access Facility		• Reduction of transmission of COVID-19 across borders (doses for 22 million Bangladeshis) • Quicker reduction in barriers to exports, imports, and investments • Supports upgrading the interoperability of vaccine-related IT systems to improve tracking and monitoring of vaccines, cold chain and logistics	• Harmonization with WHO approaches, standards, and tools

CAREC = Central Asia Regional Economic Cooperation, COVID-19 = coronavirus disease, COVAX = COVID-19 Vaccines Global Access, RCI = regional cooperation and integration, TA = technical assistance, WHO = World Health Organization.

[a] ADB placed on hold its assistance in Afghanistan effective 15 August 2021. https://www.adb.org/news/adb-statement-afghanistan.

Source: ADB.

Coordination and alignment with, and support for subregional cooperation and integration programs and regional organizations to combat COVID-19. It was essential that ADB's planning and delivery of RCI operations in response to COVID-19 be undertaken in close consultation with each DMC and through engagement with

---

[14]   ADB placed on hold its assistance in Afghanistan effective 15 August 2021. https://www.adb.org/news/adb-statement-afghanistan.

ADB-supported subregional cooperation programs[15] and regional cooperation organizations.[16] ADB's initiatives had to be responsive to the Asia and Pacific region's COVID-19 transition and recovery strategies, such as the ASEAN Comprehensive Recovery Framework (Box 10).

Box 10: The ASEAN Comprehensive Recovery Framework

The Association of Southeast Asian Nations (ASEAN) Comprehensive Recovery Framework was adopted at the virtual 37th ASEAN Summit on 12 November 2020, chaired by Viet Nam. The framework and the associated implementation plan serve as a strategy and coordinating mechanism for coronavirus disease (COVID-19) recovery efforts, enabling ASEAN to become more resilient and stronger in the aftermath of the COVID-19 crisis, considering the circumstances of the hardest-hit sectors and vulnerable groups. The framework focuses on five expansive strategies: (i) improving the health system, (ii) strengthening human security, (iii) maximizing the potential of the intra-ASEAN market and broader economic integration, (iv) accelerating inclusive digital transformation, and (v) advancing toward a more sustainable and resilient future. The summit emphasized that the framework's success would entail support and contributions from many stakeholders, internal and external.

Source: ASEAN Viet Nam 2020. Chairman's Statement of the 37th ASEAN Summit: Cohesive and Responsive. https://www.asean2020.vn/xem-chi-tiet1/-/asset_publisher/ynfWm23dDfpd/content/chairman-s-statement-of-the-37th-asean-summit-cohesive-and-responsive.

On regional public health matters, ADB's support for the subregional frameworks' management of the pandemic was delivered to implement their commitment and action to coordinate national responses and development with interdisciplinary and multisector approaches. The CAREC, the GMS, the SASEC, and the Pacific Islands Forum and the Council of Regional Organizations of the Pacific, with assistance from ADB and other development partners, undertook vital and innovative cross-border initiatives to respond to the COVID-19 emergency by, for example, advising on regional public health and providing technical and financial assistance to supplement resources of countries and strengthen their capabilities (Table 2).

On economic response, ADB supported countries through various RCI subregional platforms cooperating to keep borders open to trade and ensure trade facilitation. Together with development partners, ADB provided knowledge and technical services to support SMEs' continued participation in regional and global supply chains, reinforce macroeconomic and finance sector stability, and promote economic recovery (Table 3).

---

[15]   For example, the GMS and the CAREC and SASEC programs.
[16]   For example, ASEAN and the Pacific Islands Forum.

Table 2: Subregional Cooperation and Integration Programs' Public Health Response to COVID-19

Areas of Collective Action	Subregional/Country-Led Initiatives	ADB Support
• Maintaining essential health services and systems	The Pacific Island Forum established the Pacific Humanitarian Pathway on COVID-19 (PHP-C), which coordinates the intercountry movement of medical supplies and technical experts, supported by a regional task force.	Grant financing for COVID-19 testing kits. Emergency response loans for the health services sectors.
• Surveillance, infection prevention and control	GMS Working Group on Health Cooperation 'extraordinary meeting' (February 2020) for planning effective responses to COVID-19 both at the regional and country levels, and coordination with the ASEAN Secretariat. The Working Group on Health Cooperation mobilized networks from ongoing GMS health security projects for a rapid response to the pandemic.	Emergency response loans to raising capacity of health systems to WHO standards, regional information sharing and surveillance on health. The TA for the health systems' resilience and capacity for epidemic response and procurement of diagnostic and laboratory equipment.
• Regional coordination, planning, and monitoring	CAREC-wide daily reporting of new cases, sharing information on COVID-19 practices, and intercountry provision of medical teams and relief equipment.	Support for CAREC health scoping study identifying key areas for regional cooperation. Regional TAs to address regional health threats, including formulating a CAREC health strategy for improving health systems and health security capacities.

ADB = Asian Development Bank, ASEAN = Association of Southeast Asian Nations, CAREC = Central Asia Regional Economic Cooperation, COVID-19 = coronavirus disease, GMS = Greater Mekong Subregion, TA = technical assistance, WHO = World Health Organization.
Source: ADB.

Table 3: Subregional Cooperation and Integration Programs Tackle Trade, Investment, and Mobility in Response to COVID-19

Areas of Collective Action	Subregional/Country-Led Initiatives	ADB Support
• Keep borders open, ensure flow of goods	SASEC Customs Subgroup agreed to inter-agency and cross-border coordination, instituting special regimes for sensitive/critical goods.	Shared with the SASEC Customs Administrations guidelines on how customs can respond to the COVID crisis. Provided global tools and advices to customs administrations.
• Sustaining inclusive economic activity	The Pacific Humanitarian Pathway on COVID-19 (PHP-C) recognized need to sustain trade-related economic activities of MSMEs and ensure gender equality	Emergency assistance packages including support for the tradable sectors to cope with fall in economic demand, maintain export capabilities, and rebound from COVID-19.
• Fiscal policy and macroeconomic management, strengthening disaster risk management	CAREC High-Level Virtual Panel on Countercyclical Fiscal Measures for Recovery and CAREC Economic and Financial Stability Forum foster coordinated policy solutions at regional and global levels.	ADB- and/or development partner-convened knowledge events for planning fiscal policy and macroeconomic consolidation and achieving financial stability for recovery in CAREC economies.

ADB = Asian Development Bank; CAREC = Central Asia Regional Economic Cooperation; COVID-19 = coronavirus disease; MSMEs = micro, small, and medium-sized enterprises; SASEC = South Asia Subregional Economic Cooperation.
Source: ADB.

Organic Vegetable Value Chains.
Farmers from the Kalasin-Khao Kho
Organic Agricultural Cluster displaying
their produce (photo by ADB).

VII. SUSTAINING ADB'S REGIONAL COOPERATION AND INTEGRATION LEADERSHIP THROUGH KNOWLEDGE AND ADVOCACY

ADB's leadership in RCI through agenda setting and advocacy. ADB's RCI leadership among development partners in the Asia and Pacific region is, in no small part, premised on its capacity to generate knowledge and to share and advocate its use early and widely. The Operational Plan for Regional Cooperation and Integration, 2016–2020 stated that ADB would conduct knowledge work for RCI operations in partnership with centers of excellence to foster RCI-supportive policies, build cooperation agreements, and expand the sector and thematic scope of ADB's RCI-related knowledge operations, helping develop the RCI pipeline.[17] Subsequently, OP7 affirmed that ADB would strengthen its RCI expertise in areas such as (i) cross-border energy markets and energy trade agreements, (ii) multimodal transport, (iii) cross-border cooperation to help DMCs implement their nationally determined contributions under COP 21 in accordance with internationally agreed cooperative approaches and mechanisms, and (iv) the use of spatial data and methods of economic analysis to determine wider economic benefits of economic corridors.[18]

Monitoring RCI in Asia and the Pacific with ADB's improved Regional Cooperation and Integration Index (ARCII). The unprecedented global and regional development context and emerging trends affirm the importance of assessing (i) RCI's dynamics and interdependence in the Asia and Pacific region and (ii) cross-border factors supporting growth and development. The assessment requires indicators that enable policy makers to measure progress on RCI and to evaluate performance against objectives. ADB introduced the ARCII in 2017, then revised it to respond to the need for improved measures and wider coverage of RCI. As opportunities for RCI evolve, the ARCII structure is updated to include new cross-border metrics. Developing superior metrics allows researchers and policy makers to balance the

[17]   ADB. 2016. *Operational Plan for Regional Cooperation and Integration, 2016–2020*. Manila, para. 23.
[18]   ADB. 2019. *Strategy 2030 Operational Plan for Priority 7: Fostering Regional Cooperation and Integration, 2019–2024*. Manila, para. 48.

costs and benefits of RCI policies in finer detail. The ARCII's improved framework seeks to align with, complement, and assess efforts to implement the OP7's three pillars: connectivity, trade and investment, and regional public goods (RPGs).

The latest ARCII framework is presented in Figure 18, with improved coverage and data quality of the index by expanding from 158 to 173 economies, including a new subregion (the Pacific), and filling data gaps for several countries. The earlier six-dimensional framework now includes two more dimensions for assessing RCI: technology and digital connectivity, and environmental cooperation. The framework encompasses seven new indicators in existing dimensions to improve the measurement of financial integration, movement of people, and regional value chains, among others. Building on several years of experience applying ARCII to policy and associated research, ADB is considering some alternatives to the measurement approach, for example, to improve the quality of subregional analysis.

Figure 18: Improved Asia and Pacific Regional Cooperation and Integration Index Framework

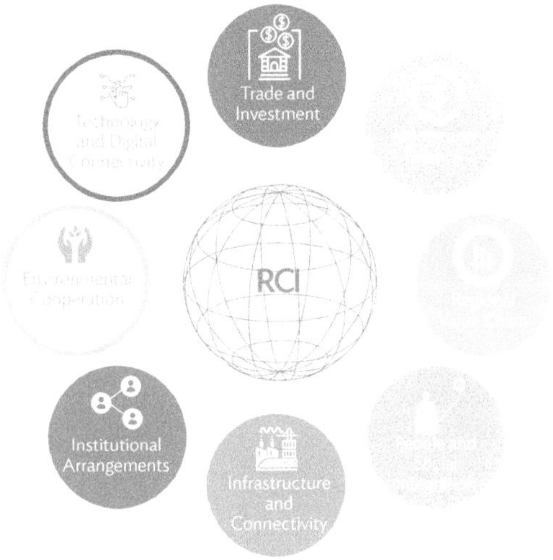

RCI = regional cooperation and integration.
Source: ADB.

Operational RCI knowledge and advisory support for upstream project development, and RCI agenda and capacity development. ADB supported the DMCs' efforts to identify and leverage RCI opportunities based on global, regional, and sector and thematic analyses, followed by upstream business development research. The RCI-TG has focused its trend analysis and business research on nonsovereign inter-subregional RCI to expand the RCI portfolio under OP7's Pillar 2: trade and investment. The intention is to diversify and increase cross-border flows of goods, services, finance, data and information, and people, while opening long-distance markets to SMEs and attracting greater inter-subregional foreign direct investment and associated technology transfer (Box 11). The approach complements other knowledge-based operational work of the operations departments and other Strategy 2030 operational priorities, such as sustainable tourism and agribusiness value chains involving cross-border flows that extend beyond a single subregion.[19]

[19] ADB. 2018. *Agricultural Value Chain Development in Selected Asian Countries: Technical Assistance Report.* Manila.

Box 11: Cross-Border Trade and Cooperation between Indonesia and Timor-Leste

Cross-border challenges and opportunities. A scoping study highlighted several opportunities for cross-border cooperation, identifying tourism and livestock as having the greatest potential. In the seven districts along the border between East Nusa Tenggara (NTT) in Indonesia and Timor-Leste, 90% of households are smallholder livestock raisers. Robust livestock demand in NTT and Timor-Leste indicates the market potential for trade of cattle from Timor-Leste to Indonesia and the expansion of poultry trade from NTT to Timor-Leste. Tourism is an important and growing income generator for NTT and Timor-Leste and could expand by building on the success of nearby Bali and cross-border tourism. Several challenges, however, reduce or eliminate the potential livelihood gains for people in both countries. Among the most pressing is the poor aviation policy environment, which reduces connectivity and raises ticket prices. Lack of agreements on the movement of vehicles across the border makes procedures burdensome and lengthy. Time-release studies revealed that border procedures are not standardized or harmonized, leading to higher costs and delays that are detrimental to the trade of perishable items such as agricultural produce.

Knowledge and support technical assistance objective, impact, and outcome. The objective of the technical assistance is to deal with the most immediate policy and capacity challenges and build the foundation for larger government and private sector investments to resolve long-term problems. The impact of the technical assistance will be more cross-border trade and investment between NTT and Timor-Leste. The outcome will be a better enabling environment between NTT and Timor-Leste for cross-border livestock trade and tourism cooperation.

Outputs, Methods, and Activities

Output 1: Knowledge of and capacity for cross-border transport and trade strengthened. The technical assistance will seek to reduce the policy and capacity barriers to cross-border trade and transport by supporting cross-border transport agreements. The technical assistance will provide policy advice to Timor-Leste on visa reform, particularly on assisting cross-border tourism, and help review the regulatory and legislative environment for cross-border air connectivity, particularly lessons learned from the Association of Southeast Asian Nations Open Skies policy.

Output 2: Animal health requirements for livestock trade bolstered. NTT must be assessed and certified as free from avian influenza. ADB will support Timor-Leste's application as being free from foot-and-mouth disease to the World Organisation for Animal Health and recommend joint surveillance and assessment of brucellosis in cattle in Timor-Leste.

Output 3: Potential joint tourism itineraries identified. ADB will achieve the output in partnership with the government, individual tour operators, and tourism and business organizations such as the Hotel Owners Association of Timor-Leste and the chambers of commerce of NTT and Timor-Leste. The technical assistance will emphasize supporting tourism that aligns with Indonesia's and Timor-Leste's Sustainable Development Goals, particularly environmental protection and gender equality. The output will build the foundation for a comprehensive strategy of joint tourism promotion and help define the needs of long-term infrastructure investment (e.g., water and sanitation in community-based tourism attractions) and workforce training.

Source: ADB. 2019. *Technical Assistance to the Cross-Border Trade and Cooperation between Indonesia and Timor-Leste.* Manila. https://www.adb.org/sites/default/files/project-documents/53111/53111-001-tar-en.pdf.

RCI conference, 2017. In November 2017, RCI Week included a 2-day roundtable conference—*Accelerating RCI in Asia and the Pacific for Economic Growth, Shared Prosperity, and Sustainability*—which focused on how economic corridors and cross-border economic zones deliver economic benefits in the Asia and Pacific region. The conference showed how economic corridor development has evolved from being focused mainly on investment in single-modal transport infrastructure to being much more holistic. The conference considered how complementary public and private sector investment across sectors and subsectors, sequenced policy reforms, urban development that encourages business clusters, institutional and skills development, and more sophisticated socioeconomic analyses can enable an economic corridor to generate and deliver diverse development benefits more widely and to sundry stakeholders.

RCI deep-dive workshop, Asia Clean Energy Forum, 2019. The 1-day workshop focused on trends and lessons learned from cross-border energy markets in Asia and elsewhere; opportunities, challenges, and priorities for further development of cross-border energy markets and energy trade in Asia, including conventional and renewable energy sources; ways to scale up investment in new cross-border energy projects in Asia and the Pacific and definition of the roles of the public and private sectors and development partners; and how to strengthen RCI as a key perspective and element in ADB's energy operations.[20]

RCI conference, 2019. In November 2019, ADB held a conference to identify regional and global trends and technological innovation impacting RCI, explore opportunities and innovative approaches to implementing the three OP7 pillars, and consider the practicality and benefits of using geographic information system (GIS) and spatial-based technology to deliver RCI operations and assess their development effectiveness. The conference considered ways for development partners to cooperate on RCI project mapping and project information databases, and the use of GIS and spatial-based data collection and analysis for upstream RCI operational planning and project design and for downstream RCI project monitoring and evaluation. Such joint activities could improve the quality of evidence on how RCI projects generate economic and social environmental benefits across and within countries.

---

[20]   Asia Clean Energy Forum 2019: *Deep Dive Workshop on Regional Cooperation and Integration (RCI) for Cross-Border Energy Markets, 21 June 2019*, Manila.

Aerial view of Danang Port.
The Port is the third largest port system
in Viet Nam and lies at the eastern
end of the GMS East–West Economic
Corridor (EWEC) (photo by ADB).

VIII. RESULTS FROM COMPLETED REGIONAL COOPERATION AND INTEGRATION OPERATIONS

RCI is included in ADB's Corporate Results Framework (CRF) at various levels, reported in ADB annual Development Effectiveness Reviews (DEfRs). Asia and the Pacific's progress on RCI as a broad impact measure is assessed using Level 1 indicators, and the outcome performance of ADB's RCI operations is assessed using Level 2 indicators, supplemented by information on associated tracking or subpillar indicators in the OP7 results framework (Appendix 2). A summary of RCI results as reported in the 2020 and 2019 DEfR is given in Figure 19, showing the changes caused by COVID-19 as well as the adoption of the new Strategy 2030 RCI OP7.

Figure 19: Highlights of Operational Priority 7 Results at Levels 1 and 2
in the ADB Development Effectiveness Reviews, 2020 and 2019

Development Effectiveness Review, 2020

Levels 1 and 2 Results

Share of ADB Projects
Aligned with OP7

OP7 FOSTERING REGIONAL COOPERATION AND INTEGRATION

ARCII

ARCII Index
0.45 in 2018
0   0.44 in 2017   1

Asia-Pacific Regional Cooperation and
Integration Index scores improved,
but countries prioritized national measures
to manage the pandemic

$1.37B INVESTMENTS trade and investment *facilitated*

66 Measures to improve execution of new or existing trade or investment agreements *supported*

8 Measures to develop existing or new cross-border economic corridors *supported*

1 INITIATIVE regional public goods *initiative*

7 Measures to improve regional public health and education services *supported in implementation*

12 Regional or subregional mechanisms *operationalized* to enhance DMC cooperation in trade, finance, or multisector economic corridors

OP7
29%

continued on next page

Figure 19 *continued*

OP7 = Strategy 2030 Operational Priority 7: Fostering Regional Cooperation and Integration.

Source: ADB.

More detailed information on Level 2 results is presented in Figure 20, showing alignment with Sustainable Development Goals (SDGs) as well as outcome achievements in ADB's performance against respective targets.

Figure 20: Level 2 Indicators, Development Effectiveness Review, 2019

Indicator	SDG	Number of Completion Reports PCR / XARR / TCR	Results Achieved	Achievement Rate (%)	Signal
7.1 Cargo transported and energy transmitted across borders ($)	17	1	219,300,000	100	✓
7.2 Trade and investment facilitated ($)	17	3	237,434,000	100+	✓
7.3 Regional public goods initiatives successfully reducing cross-border environmental or health risks, or providing regional access to education services (number)	17	1 1	3	100	
7.1 Cargo transported and energy transmitted across borders ($)	17			–	
7.2 Trade and investment facilitated ($)	17	3	237,434,000	100+	✓
7.3 Regional public goods initiatives successfully reducing cross-border environmental or health risks, or providing regional access to education services (number)	17	1 1	3	100	

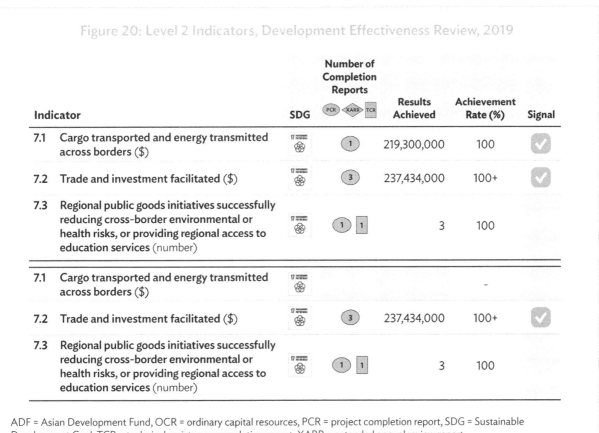

ADF = Asian Development Fund, OCR = ordinary capital resources, PCR = project completion report, SDG = Sustainable Development Goal, TCR = technical assistance completion report, XARR = extended annual review report.

Source: ADB.

The outcome performance is supplemented by tracking indicators with SDG alignment (Figure 21). The results for the 12 tracking indicators (DEfR 2019) show that ADB's RCI operations have been (i) expanding cross-border trade in clean energy, (ii) strengthening cross-border coordination mechanisms enabling trade, finance, and multisector economic corridors, and other mechanisms to coordinate RPGs, (iii) supporting efficiency and productivity of other, large investments in cross-border connectivity, and (iv) helping improve regional health and education and execute trade agreements. However, the tracking results indicate that ADB's RCI needs to make greater efforts to enable more cross-border collaboration on ICT, broader financial cooperation, and cross-border protection of the environment and natural resources.

Figure 21: Tracking Indicators, Development Effectiveness Review, 2019
(ADB Operations Overall)

Indicator		Results Achieved
7.1.1	Transport and ICT connectivity assets established or improved (number)	6
7.1.2	Measures to improve the efficiency and/or productivity of cross-border connectivity supported in implementation (number)	16
7.1.3	Clean energy capacity for power trade installed or improved (megawatt equivalent)	1,000
7.1.4	Regional or subregional mechanisms created or operationalized to enhance coordination and cooperation among DMCs in energy, transport, or ICT connectivity (number)	1
7.2.1	Measures to improve execution of provisions in existing or new trade or investment agreements supported in implementation (number)	8
7.2.2	Measures to develop existing and/or new cross-border economic corridors supported in implementation (number)	3
7.2.3	Measures to improve regional financial cooperation supported in implementation (number)	2
7.2.4	Regional or subregional mechanisms created or operationalized to enhance coordination and cooperation among DMCs in trade, finance, or multisector economic corridors (number)	23
7.3.1	Measures to improve shared capacity of DMCs to mitigate or adapt to climate change supported in implementation (number)	1
7.3.2	Measures to expand cross-border environmental protection and sustainable management of shared natural resources supported in implementation (number)	–
7.3.3	Measures to improve regional public health and education services supported in implementation (number)	9
7.3.4	Regional or subregional mechanisms created or operationalized to enhance coordination and cooperation among DMCs on regional public goods (number)	10

DMC = developing member country, ICT = information and communication technology, PCR = project completion report, SDG = Sustainable Development Goal, TCR = technical assistance completion report, XARR = extended annual review report.

Note: Results delivered as reported in PCRs, XARRs, and TCRs circulated from 1 January to 15 November 2019. Values smaller than 1,000 are rounded to the nearest 10. Values smaller than 99 are not rounded.

Source: ADB.

Taken together, the results are encouraging. The region's progress on RCI is stable or slightly increasing, ADB's RCI operations are achieving their outcome targets through supporting more cross-border flows of cargo and energy, and the value of facilitated trade and investment continues to increase. Some of the results achieved by projects meet or exceed the planned results, as indicated by the achievement rates reported in the DEfRs.

It is noteworthy that while RCI remains one of the seven Operational Priorities (OPs), the corporate target for its operations has been discontinued, indicating a shift from measuring inputs (RCI lending share) to outcomes (Level 2 CRF). In recent pre-pandemic years, the share of OP7 investment projects in ADB-wide annual commitments was stable below its then-target of 30%, but the DEfR 2019 showed their satisfactory performance to achieve outcome targets. With the RCI scorecard (as discussed in Chapter VIII) to strengthen the RCI quality of project classification, ADB's RCI operations need to be further enhanced—at least at the planning and implementing phases using possible relevant tracking indicators like number and/or volumes of RCI-classified project approvals and commitments, in order to better promote a more expansive agenda of cross-border development activities and a broader range of cross-border cooperation among DMCs (see Chapter X).

RCI projects performance validated by the Independent Evaluation Department (IED).[21] In recent years, completed RCI operations of the Central and West Asia Department (CWRD), East Asia Department (EARD), South Asia Department, and Southeast Asia Department (SERD), and in Bangladesh, Cambodia, Georgia, Kazakhstan, the Lao People's Democratic Republic, Nepal, Pakistan, the People's Republic of China (PRC), Thailand, Turkmenistan, and Uzbekistan were mostly rated successful. The projects covered energy, finance, industry and trade, public sector management, and transport; eased participation of and delivered benefits to women, ethnic minorities, and SMEs, among others; stimulated trade in new local products; and helped develop the private sector. These evaluations were generally validated by IED confirming the projects' performances. Several of the IED validations for the period 2017–2020 are presented in Appendix 3.

----

[21]   Each year ADB's IED validates project completion reports, including those for RCI loan and grant operations.

The Trade Gate on Pakistani side.
ADB's Central Asia and Regional Economic Cooperation Programme strives to create and encourage positive atmosphere for trade between borders (photo by ADB).

IX. STRENGTHENING REGIONAL COOPERATION AND INTEGRATION PROJECT QUALITY, RESOURCE MOBILIZATION, AND HUMAN RESOURCE DEVELOPMENT

Strengthening Regional Cooperation and Integration Project Quality through Systematic Scorecard Assessment

RCI project classification and scorecard. To institutionalize the RCI OP (OP7) to ensure quality of RCI operations, in 2020 a set of RCI institutional documents were approved, the Operations Manual B1 on RCI, supported by a Staff Instruction on Business Process for RCI and a Guidance Note on RCI Scorecard, developed by the RCI-TG Secretariat. All proposed RCI loan and TA projects are assessed using the RCI scorecard (Figure 22). The operations departments must complete the scorecard, providing as much detail as possible, and propose actions that will generate further evidence later in project preparation. Loan, grant, or TA proposals that cannot meet the scorecard's requirements will not qualify for further processing under the RCI classification. However, the project team can modify the project design to strengthen its adherence to different sections of the scorecard, and the project design may then be further assessed. Operations departments apply the RCI project classification in line with the scorecard criteria, to be expedited by ADB's in-house training program on RCI project classification, associated economic analysis, and other relevant knowledge work. The project's scorecard may be revised and updated during circulation of the draft TA report or loan and grant report and recommendation of the President to the Board of Directors.

Internal and online training modules on the RCI scorecard were developed and delivered to key RCI staff in the community as well as relevant sector groups, including transport. As staff gained experience in applying the scorecard, the RCI-TG Secretariat and sector and thematic units in the regional departments engaged in wider and more systematic dialogue, operations staff received more regular and uniform RCI economics training, and the link between upstream RCI project preparation knowledge work and the subsequent design of the ensuing RCI loan and grant was strengthened.

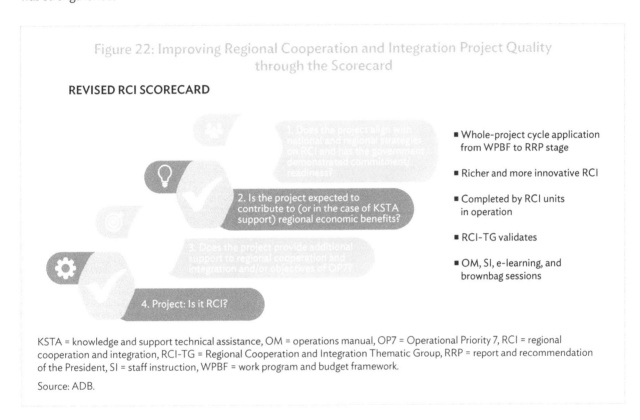

Figure 22: Improving Regional Cooperation and Integration Project Quality through the Scorecard

REVISED RCI SCORECARD

1. Does the project align with national and regional strategies on RCI and has the government demonstrated commitment/readiness?

2. Is the project expected to contribute to (or in the case of KSTA support) regional economic benefits?

3. Does the project provide additional support to regional cooperation and integration and/or objectives of OP7?

4. Project: Is it RCI?

- Whole-project cycle application from WPBF to RRP stage
- Richer and more innovative RCI
- Completed by RCI units in operation
- RCI-TG validates
- OM, SI, e-learning, and brownbag sessions

KSTA = knowledge and support technical assistance, OM = operations manual, OP7 = Operational Priority 7, RCI = regional cooperation and integration, RCI-TG = Regional Cooperation and Integration Thematic Group, RRP = report and recommendation of the President, SI = staff instruction, WPBF = work program and budget framework.

Source: ADB.

Mobilizing External and Internal Financial Resources to Support Regional Cooperation and Integration

RCI Special Funds

A number of funding sources dedicated for RCI operations were managed to provide untied grants for advisory, project preparatory, and regional TA. The Regional Cooperation and Integration Financing Partnership Facility (February 2007) to channel financing and knowledge resources from development partners in support of ADB's RCI program comprises three funds: (i) the multi-donor Regional Cooperation and Integration Fund (RCIF), (ii) the Investment Climate Facilitation Fund, and (iii) the Asia Regional Trade and Connectivity Fund. The People's Republic of China Poverty Reduction and Regional Cooperation Fund (March 2005) also finances activities to reduce poverty, promote regional cooperation, and boost knowledge sharing in ADB DMCs.[22] A snapshot of these special funds' mobilized resources and their allocation as of the end of 2019 is given in Figure 23.

----

[22] ADB supports the RCIF. Japan supports the Investment Climate Facilitation Fund. The United Kingdom supports the Asia Regional Trade and Connectivity Fund. The PRC supports the People's Republic of China Poverty Reduction and Regional Cooperation Fund.

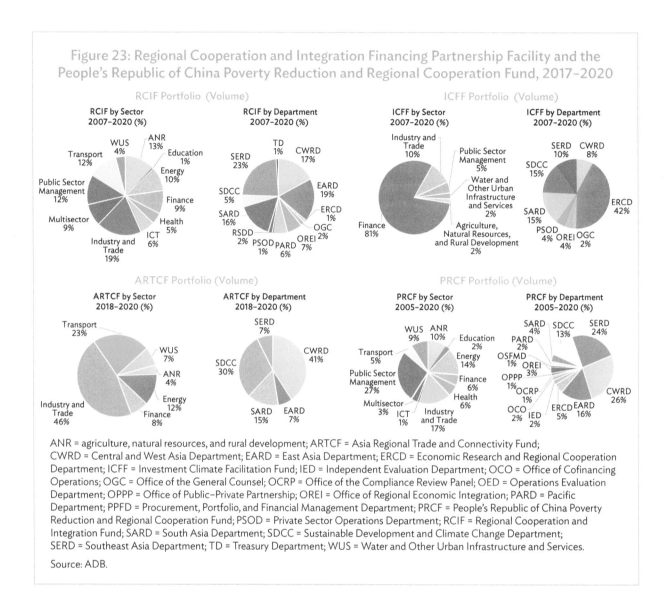

Figure 23: Regional Cooperation and Integration Financing Partnership Facility and the People's Republic of China Poverty Reduction and Regional Cooperation Fund, 2017–2020

ANR = agriculture, natural resources, and rural development; ARTCF = Asia Regional Trade and Connectivity Fund; CWRD = Central and West Asia Department; EARD = East Asia Department; ERCD = Economic Research and Regional Cooperation Department; ICFF = Investment Climate Facilitation Fund; IED = Independent Evaluation Department; OCO = Office of Cofinancing Operations; OGC = Office of the General Counsel; OCRP = Office of the Compliance Review Panel; OED = Operations Evaluation Department; OPPP = Office of Public–Private Partnership; OREI = Office of Regional Economic Integration; PARD = Pacific Department; PPFD = Procurement, Portfolio, and Financial Management Department; PRCF = People's Republic of China Poverty Reduction and Regional Cooperation Fund; PSOD = Private Sector Operations Department; RCIF = Regional Cooperation and Integration Fund; SARD = South Asia Department; SDCC = Sustainable Development and Climate Change Department; SERD = Southeast Asia Department; TD = Treasury Department; WUS = Water and Other Urban Infrastructure and Services.

Source: ADB.

Performance evaluation of the RCIF, 2007–2019. In the first half of 2020, ADB's IED disseminated the findings of its performance evaluation for the RCIF.[23] It found that the RCIF achieved its key objective and had potential to further promote ADB's RCI agenda. The fund is aligned with ADB's RCI strategy and the related operational plans and has provided additional financial support for RCI activities, particularly in cross-border trade facilitation and cooperation on RPGs. The RCIF has produced usable knowledge products, including regional strategies and master plans, and provided a platform for knowledge and experience sharing for policy and capacity development. The overall fund management and administration have been efficient and TA processes have seen some improvement in recent years. Overall, the evaluation assessed the RCIF as successful, relevant, effective, and efficient, although, given its need for continued and almost exclusive ADB support, less than likely sustainable. The evaluation recommended that ADB Management (i) introduce measures to ensure better monitoring of progress and achievement of RCIF objectives and (ii) strengthen engagement with resident missions and national counterparts, including the private sector where applicable.

....

[23]   ADB. 2020. *Regional Cooperation and Integration Fund, 2007–2019*. Manila.

RCI Set-Aside under the Asian Development Fund 13 Thematic Pool

The Asian Development Fund (ADF) 13 thematic pool, commenced in 2020, provide grant funding for investment project in three priorities, one of which is fostering RCI with a focus on RPGs for concession-eligible DMCs. Resources are allocated to projects through an annual project submission and selection process using a two-step approach:

(i)   Projects must meet eligibility criteria for Group A and B countries under the ADF.[24] Projects under any of the OP7 pillars—connectivity, trade and investment, and RPGs—are eligible in Group A countries, but only projects related to Pillar 3 (RPGs) are eligible in Group B countries.

(ii)   The eligible projects are scored according to the following criteria, which rely on performance-based indicators and have different weights. A higher score is considered if the projects (a) are in countries with prudent or improved fiscal, debt, and budget management; (b) have high development RCI impact; (c) are in countries with better country portfolio performance; (d) are multicountry and multi-thematic; (e) leverage external funding or have more buy-in of the government; (f) are innovative; and (g) take place in fragile and conflict-affected situations or small island developing states.

Table 4 sets out the ADF 13 Thematic Pool eligibility framework.

Table 4: Project Eligibility Criteria for Regional Cooperation and Integration and Regional Public Good Projects in the Asian Development Fund Thematic Pool

Group A Countries	Group B Countries
Stand-alone projects and discrete project components and/or outputs pertaining to the three strategic priorities outlined in the RCI Operational Plan for 2019–2024 are eligible if they have (i) greater and higher-quality connectivity between economies, (ii) expanded global and regional trade and investment opportunities, and (iii) increased and diversified RPGs. Focus will be on environmental protection and sustainable management of shared natural resources, including ocean health, biodiversity and ecosystem services, and regional health security. All projects must have been classified as RCI following assessment through the RCI scorecard. The scorecard considers the (i) relevance of the project to regional agreements and strategies; (ii) existence of cross-border economic spillovers; and (iii) wider benefits such as regional harmonization of standards, technology transfer, and knowledge sharing.	Stand-alone projects and discrete project components and/or outputs pertaining only to "increased and diversified RPGs" are eligible. Focus will be given to environmental protection and sustainable management of shared natural resources, which include ocean health, biodiversity and ecosystem services, and regional health security. Only projects in Group B countries with prudent (average score of relevant CPA criteria is above 3 out of 6) or improved fiscal, debt, and budget management (average score of relevant CPA criteria has increased) will be eligible.

CPA = country performance assessment, RCI = regional cooperation and integration, RPG = regional public good.

Source: Asian Development Bank.

----

24   Countries in Group A receive only concessional assistance and those in Group B a blend of ordinary capital resources and concessional assistance.

In June 2020, regional departments submitted 42 projects in response to the first call for proposals for the ADF 13 thematic pool. An internal committee of staff from the SDCC and the SPD assessed and scored each proposal based on a set of eligibility criteria for each strategic area and on a set of selection criteria. The cross-technical reviews of proposals by thematic experts from regional departments informed the assessments. In 2020, a total of 29 projects were selected for financing in 2021–2022, totaling $291 million, of which $158 million (54%) was allocated to finance proposals for RCI RPG projects.

Cofinancing for RCI-Classified Projects

Loans, grants, and technical assistance. In 2017–2020, cofinancing for RCI operations amounted to $4.235 billion, of which $4.172 billion (98.5%) was mobilized for loan and grant operations and $0.062 billion (1.5%) for TA operations (Figure 24). The trend for TA cofinancing is "flat;" greater efforts need to be made to improve this trend through closer operational-level collaboration with bilateral and multilateral partners including support for implementing RCI activities under established RCI subregional programs and other regional cooperation entities. There was no clear trend for loan and grant operations; the pattern of RCI cofinancing for loan and grant operations continues to be driven mainly by individual project opportunities rather than a strategic programmatic approach for RCI cofinancing with other development partners. Going forward, a more strategic programmatic approach should be considered, again under the framework of established RCI subregional programs and other regional entities.

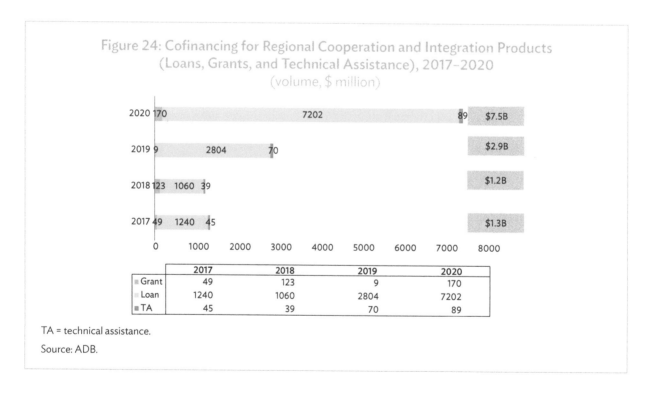

Figure 24: Cofinancing for Regional Cooperation and Integration Products
(Loans, Grants, and Technical Assistance), 2017–2020
(volume, $ million)

	2017	2018	2019	2020
Grant	49	123	9	170
Loan	1240	1060	2804	7202
TA	45	39	70	89

TA = technical assistance.

Source: ADB.

Human Resource and Skills Development

RCI skills registry and survey. In late 2017, the RCI-TG, in cooperation with the BPMSD, updated the technical skills registry for RCI and, in early 2018, conducted an ADB-wide RCI skills survey (self-assessment), which enumerated the number of staff with 15 defined RCI skills and their proficiency (Figure 25). The results demonstrated that

RCI human resource and skills development needed to prioritize (i) minimizing the number of staff holding only foundational RCI skills and raising their proficiency to at least intermediate level, (ii) raising the proficiency of staff with intermediate skills to advanced level, and (iii) raising the proficiency of RCI skills in a number of sector operational areas.

RCI skills development and acquisition. Post-survey, RCI skills development has proceeded along three lines: (i) ADB plus development partner knowledge sharing and knowledge networking events focused on RCI innovations and their current and potential application across many sector and thematic areas and in differentiated regional, subregional, and country contexts;[25] (ii) presentations by the RCI-TG Secretariat and operations departments on the methodologies, technologies, and outputs of upstream business research for RCI pipeline development;[26] and (iii) specialized training, particularly RCI economic analysis and the application of the RCI scorecard for project classification.[27] At the time of writing, the Strategic Workforce Unit (BPOD-SWU) is currently working on skills inventory of positions in ADB and is seeking SDCC's assistance to determine the skill/s of positions, specifically those relating to sector and thematic areas, including RCI. The RCI-TG has canvased inputs from operations departments and the results are being consolidated. Indicative RCI operational skills priorities include, among others: competitiveness in connected markets, connectivity between economies, cross-border infrastructure, economics and knowledge management, geopolitical situation analysis, RPGs and collective action, and regulatory/legal expertise for RCI.

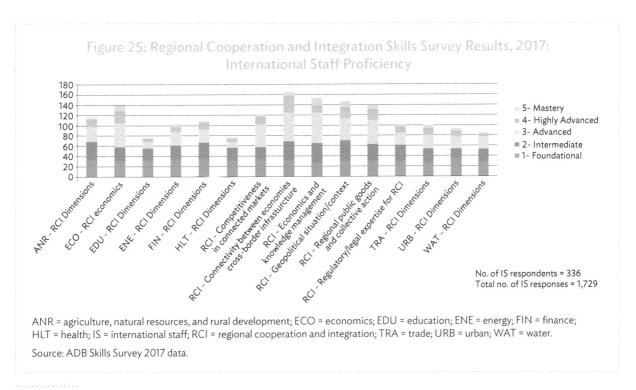

Figure 25: Regional Cooperation and Integration Skills Survey Results, 2017: International Staff Proficiency

No. of IS respondents = 336
Total no. of IS responses = 1,729

ANR = agriculture, natural resources, and rural development; ECO = economics; EDU = education; ENE = energy; FIN = finance; HLT = health; IS = international staff; RCI = regional cooperation and integration; TRA = trade; URB = urban; WAT = water.

Source: ADB Skills Survey 2017 data.

---

25   At the Digital Development Forum during ADB Digital Week 2019, the RCI-TG held a session for ADB staff on ways to foster new digital technologies under the OP7 pillars (e.g., use new digital technologies to make connectivity infrastructure more productive, expand regional and global market access in the services trade for SMEs, and expand cross-border access of the poor and vulnerable to specialized health services).

26   For example, in mid-2018, presenting the draft final report of the Indonesia–Timor-Leste Cross-Border Zone Study and the draft interim country reports (India, Thailand, and Cambodia) for the India–Mekong SME Internationalization Study, the final step of internal peer review, before submitting the reports to governments and presenting them at in-country workshops in October and November 2018.

27   Preparation of the Handbook for the Classification and Economic Analysis of Regional Projects and associated staff training on methodologies to (i) identify and justify RCI projects at the concept stage and (ii) ensure that RCI project economic analysis is fully consistent with the ADB Guidelines for the Economic Analysis of Projects.

Facilitating Cross-Border Transport.
A staff at the Wagah Cargo Inspection
Terminal checks a Pakistani truck arriving
from India (photo by ADB).

X. FOSTERING RECOVERY AND RESILIENCE: WIDER, DEEPER, MORE OPEN REGIONAL COOPERATION AND INTEGRATION

The COVID-19 recovery pathway across the region is multifaceted and will demand continuous intercountry cooperation and innovative approaches to reignite cross-border flows and their contributions to national development. This requires a shared, collaborative approach to pursue coherent multisector and inter-sector measures of "building back better"—addressing not only developmental challenges but at the same time promoting inclusion, resilience, and sustainability. This can only be done with effective regional and interregional coordination, as COVID-19's volatile, uncertain, complex, and ambiguous environment is unprecedented and beyond the capabilities and resources of most individual countries to tackle on their own. Thus, strong partnership among DMCs and between them and their development partners, including ADB are vital to implement the necessary recovery measures.

Wider, deeper, more open RCI is required. With considerable foresight, in 2020, ADB Management called on countries in Asia and the Pacific and on ADB to pursue wider, deeper, and more open RCI for the region to overcome COVID-19 and emerge stronger:

- **Wider.** Expanding RCI to new and emerging areas such as regional health security, regional education services, gender and social protection, sustainable tourism development, economic migration and forced displacement, trade in renewable energy, and digital services and the platform economy promoting trade in goods. It involves focusing on the key enablers for recovery—digitization, skills and jobs, and financial sustainability.
- **Deeper.** Adopting a holistic approach considering health and other social concerns, climate change and other environmental threats, and financial stability issues; diversifying within sectors; and digitizing sector/subsector/industry technologies, operations, and systems that enable new or larger cross-border flows, for example in the finance sector in support of portable social protection for economic migrants, and for sustainable tourism.
- **More open.** Adopting more fluid and flexible approaches to collaboration that cut across, or go beyond, the prevailing "architecture" of regional and subregional groupings in order to expand the breadth and depth of policy dialogues; enlarge the space for knowledge sharing and capacity development; and pool knowledge, expertise, and other resources more efficiently and effectively. It also involves linking or aligning RCI initiatives with global, regional, and subregional frameworks, agendas, and their methods. A more open RCI would be more inclusive, involving new partners and thought leaders in the private sector, think tanks, academic institutions, and civil society organizations, while continuing to strengthen collaboration with traditional development partners.

Figure 26: Opportunities for Wider, Deeper, and More Open Regional Cooperation and Integration

Greater and higher quality connectivity between economies	Global and regional trade and investment opportunities expanded	Regional public goods increased and diversified

Wider RCI

Digitalization
- Regional mechanisms to streamline requirements for cross-border data flows
- Regional forums on challenges, issues, and policy responses to digitalization (competition, innovation access of micro-businesses, data privacy, and cybersecurity)
- Capacity building on digital solutions in different sectors

Supply chains
- Engage in deeper regional trade integration and stronger trade liberalization through mega trade deals
- Redirect investments in the green and blue economy, and services
- Transport and logistics solutions responsive to changing consumer demands
- Centralized web portals as information hubs
- Coordinated border management

Education and labor markets
- Knowledge sharing and capacity building on educational technologies
- Coordination on labor market information systems
- Harmonization of educational competencies and skills standards
- Regional frameworks for mutual recognition of educational qualifications
- Regional frameworks of online quality assurance and credentials

Gender and the care sector
- Assessment of adverse impacts of pandemic on gender
- Knowledge sharing on issues of unpaid work, community-based care, long-term care, domestic workers; public and private affordable care for children and the elderly

E-commerce
- Harmonization of technical and regulatory standards of data systems
- Capacity building on applications of digital technologies in different sectors
- Resource mobilization for technological development

Safe international mobility
- Regional framework on safe international travel
- Knowledge-sharing forum
- Harmonized practice on contact tracing, risk classification, testing, mobile health insurance, and electronic travel certificates

Disaster preparedness
- Capacity development on strengthening coordination mechanisms and communications systems for health pandemics

Financial inclusion
- Policy and regulatory cooperation on regional payments settlements
- Digital payments schemes
- Knowledge sharing, dissemination of best practices

Deeper RCI

Resilient infrastructure
- Building resilient cross-border infrastructure (risk prevention, rapid recovery, data protection and safety, etc.)
- Inclusivity for a wide range of users
- Multimodal connectivity
- Transport facilitation
- Decarbonizing transport systems

Tourism
- Regional coordination in opening borders
- Safe and seamless border management
- Use of technology for safe, seamless, and touchless travel
- Reliable, consistent, and easy access to information on travel restrictions and protocols
- Harmonize travel and tourism-related health protocols
- Promotion of low-carbon tourism
- Travel facilitation

Trade facilitation
- Joint actions on regulatory and institutional reforms based on international and regional framework agreements
- Trade information portals
- Monitoring of trade facilitation performance
- Information sharing on best practices
- Capacity building for Implementing Trade Facilitation Agreement and Revised Kyoto Convention

Low-carbon transition
- Developing integrated solutions to low-carbon transitions
- Information sharing and benchmarking
- Technological development and diffusion
- Common standards for cross-border infrastructure
- Dialogue on trade and climate change issues (e.g. carbon tax on imports)

Social protection
- Monitoring and reporting on social protection programs (Social Protection Index)
- Knowledge sharing on new themes: new vulnerabilities created by COVID-19; fiscal limitations and long-term sustainability; linking social protection to livelihood opportunities
- Capacity building for multisector actors

Renewable energy
- Regional trade in hydropower
- Harmonization of technical, institutional frameworks and tariff pricing regimes
- Dialogues on climate change impacts and social impacts associated with hydropower

Regional health security
- Soft components of health-care delivery
- Governance
- Health finance
- Cross-border registration of health workers and pooled training
- Regional buffer stocking of essential medicines
- RPGs for health

Migration
- Shared information infrastructure and migrant registration
- Dialogue on policy gaps in worker protection, risk mitigation for migrants
- Common template on streamlined procedures to acquire portability of social protection
- Knowledge sharing on best practices

More Open
- Fluid and flexible approaches that cut across or go beyond existing regional and subregional groupings
- More open platforms for policy dialogue, knowledge sharing, and capacity building
- Linking and aligning RCI interventions with global agendas and regional and subregional frameworks or initiatives
- Pooling knowledge products and resources for wider and greater efficiency of access
- Enhanced collaboration with development partners; expanded partnerships with think tanks, academic institutions, and civil society organizations

COVID-19 = coronavirus disease, RCI = regional cooperation and integration, RPG = regional public good.

Source: ADB.

Figure 26 sets out an indicative or reference framework for implementing OP7's main operational pillars for the purpose of achieving wider deeper, more open RCI that assists the region to build back better, together.[28]

Under the framework of wider, deeper, and more open RCI, ADB's three main RCI roles—honest broker, knowledge provider and capacity builder, and mobilizer of project financing—will become even more important, but they will need to evolve and adapt by, for example, embracing greater use of digital technologies, increasingly adopt multisector and theme-based "One ADB" approaches, use the full range of ADB instruments and modalities, disseminating and sharing knowledge in more innovative ways, and expanding engagement with the private sector (Figures 27 and 28).

Figure 27: Evolving and Adapting ADB's Roles to Advance Wider, Deeper, More Open Regional Cooperation and Integration in Asia and the Pacific

ADB's Three Roles in RCI Will Become Even More Important

Honest Broker	Knowledge Provider and Capacity Builder	Mobilizer of Project Financing
▪ Step up secretariat roles in subregional cooperation programs	▪ Broaden and deepen RCI knowledge/skills in emerging areas	▪ Promote domestic resource mobilization for RCI projects
▪ Strengthen coordination and catalytic role in addressing shared development issues	▪ Increase innovation in generating and disseminating knowledge	▪ Encourage higher cost-sharing by higher-income DMCs
▪ Maximize use of digital technology platform	▪ Mainstream digital innovations	▪ Expand cofinancing to invest in new sectors/subsectors
▪ Facilitate inter-subregional RCI		▪ Explore new private sector financing for cross-border investments
▪ Bring in more development partners		

ADB = Asian Development Bank, DMC = developing member country, RCI = regional cooperation and integration.
Source: ADB.

---

[28] At the time of writing, the RCI-TG circulated internally a draft guidance note, "Fostering Regional Cooperation and Integration for Recovery and Resilience," which is the source of Figure 28, and it also sets out and discusses in greater detail a range themes or issues that could be addressed under a wider, deeper, more open RCI framework and support an inclusive and sustainable post-COVID-19 recovery. For the purpose of selective illustration: EDUCATION, draw on emerging good practices from different regions on new and cross-sector approaches such as digital learning and green recovery through green skills; WATER, cross-border dialogue and agreements on cooperation to manage transboundary water resources in relation to hydropower, irrigation, fisheries, flood protection, and involve stakeholders at national and subnational levels (CAREC has recently added water as a pillar for cooperation and a strategy is being developed); and FINANCE, strengthening the observance of international financial standards, and codes, to promote greater economic and financial stability at both the domestic and regional level, and fostering the adoption of financial technology with better understanding of risks and providing cross-border financial education for access to financial services.

Figure 28: Approaches to Implement Wider, Deeper, and More Open
Regional Cooperation and Integration

Build innovative RCI pipeline ✓

- Expand upstream analytical work

- Use WPBF process to ensure incorporation of RCI priorities into pipeline

- Ensure inclusion of health sector in the RCI pipeline

Increasingly adopt multi-sector and theme-based "One ADB" approaches ✓

- Multiple sectors and themes

- Multiple countries/subregions

- New sectors/subsectors, especially those badly hit by the pandemic

Use full range of ADB instruments and modalities ✓

- Technical assistance funded by RCIF, trust funds, and corporate TA allocation

- Loans and grants (including ADF-13 Thematic Pool)

- PBL/RBL to (i) align policy and regulatory environment with emerging needs, (ii) improve coordination and cooperation among countries, and (iii) provide opportunities for the private sector participation

- Capacity building for innovation through (i) training of RD/RM staff for stronger RCI skills, (ii) strengthening of RCI network within ADB, and (iii) knowledge sharing

ADB = Asian Development Bank, ADF = Asian Development Fund, DMC = developing member country, PBL = policy-based lending, RBL = results-based lending, RCI = regional cooperation and integration, RCIF = Regional Cooperation and Integration Fund, RD = regional department, RM = resident mission, TA = technical assistance, WPBF = work program and budget framework.

Source: ADB.

Border check point on the Lao side of the Mekong River. Lao PDR and Thailand are now linked by "Friendship Bridge II" completed in 2007 (photo by ADB).

XI. CONCLUSIONS AND THE WAY FORWARD

Conclusions

This report shows that ADB's RCI operations during the period of 2017–2020 have, overall, been responsive to its RCI OP7, emerging global and regional trends, and the unprecedented cross-border challenges of the COVID-19 pandemic. The annual development effectiveness reviews show that ADB's RCI operations positively contribute to the Asia and Pacific region's progress on RCI and the Sustainable Development Goals (SDGs), and the RCI targets in the Corporate Results Framework (CRF) are generally met for this period.

The RCI portfolio balances sector and subsector diversification in investment and technical assistance (TA). The trend has been underpinned by adoption of new technologies and approaches to create more widely dispersed cross-border spillovers, achieving synergies and complementarity across the OP7's pillars: connectivity, trade and investment, and RPGs. ADB has continued to assist DMC-led subregional cooperation and integration programs and other country-led regional cooperation organizations. The support has been instrumental in achieving coherent, innovative, and timely cross-border collaboration among countries to (i) tackle the COVID-19 health emergency, (ii) leverage regional benefits from national vaccination programs, (iii) support the tradable sector more broadly, (iv) coordinate policy responses across neighboring countries, and (v) extend that cooperation into planning the transition to recovery.

ADB's support for RCI needs to expand OP7's complementarity with the other six Strategy 2030 operational priorities and thereby increase the number of RCI investment operations as a share of total ADB annual commitments, reflecting RCI's critical development role as envisaged in ADB's Charter. Greater sector and thematic diversification of the TA portfolio increases the potential of RCI operations to achieve development effectiveness in support of inclusive and sustainable post-COVID-19 recovery. The other RCI specialized knowledge operations have focused on identifying new cross-border opportunities, further RCI innovations, and improved approaches and analytics for broader and deeper understanding of RCI outcomes and impacts. ADB must apply digital technologies to all types of cross-border flows and move beyond what has so far been only a modest beginning in inter-subregional RCI operations. ADB's RCI must expand nonsovereign operations into more sector and thematic areas across borders and link sovereign and nonsovereign efforts to generate large RPGs (e.g., improved ocean health) across subregions.

ADB's RCI management innovation—through the RCI scorecard and associated staff training, including complementary training on RCI economics—is supporting RCI development effectiveness. The RCI scorecard is a systematic approach that supports alignment of projects with resources and thematic priorities and generates clearer identification of potential outcomes. Application of the scorecard is leading to better project design and monitoring frameworks and clearer identification of potential—direct and additional—outcomes. The RCI-TG Committee has diligently overseen the allocation of special fund resources by managing the ADF's RCI set-aside from the SPD and mobilizing grant funding for RCI operations through the RCI-TG Secretariat. The BPMSD, in consultation with the RCI-TG, has systematically assessed ADB's current and projected RCI skills and competency requirements.

The Way Forward

RCI loans and grants: 2022–2024 pipeline. The indicative RCI loan and grant pipeline for years 2022–2024 (Figure 29) shows both positive, but also less positive attributes. On the positive side, there is an improved balance of operations across nine key DMC economic and social sectors, which together reflect all three main operational pillars of OP7. On the less positive side, the apparent scope for capital investment in digital connectivity is small, and the amount of annual aggregate RCI commitments is back to pre-pandemic levels, as is RCI's share in the projected total annual ADB commitments, on both a volume and number of projects basis. Thus, the RCI-TG Secretariat , the RCI Thematic Committee, and the ADB-assisted RCI subregional program secretariats need to make greater and innovative efforts to identify more opportunities for integrating RCI across the full set of ADB's sector/thematic pipelines for the 2022–2024 period. In that regard it is important to note that, at the time of writing, the draft ADB Three-Year Work Program and Budget 2022–2024 has set out an unprecedented projection for the volume of ADB assistance across the region over the next 3 years. It is absolutely essential that RCI expands its participation in the development of the ensuing portfolio of ADB's operations going forward, both in terms of volume of assistance and the number of operations. The next 3 years will be a crucial "test" for ADB's RCI to expand its contribution to the post-COVID-19 recovery across Asia and the Pacific.

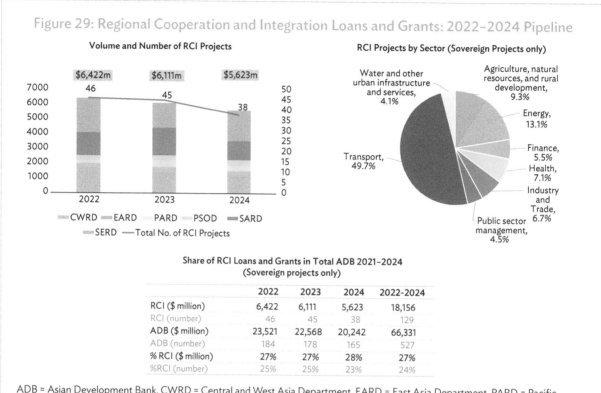

Figure 29: Regional Cooperation and Integration Loans and Grants: 2022–2024 Pipeline

Volume and Number of RCI Projects

RCI Projects by Sector (Sovereign Projects only)

Agriculture, natural resources, and rural development, 9.3%
Water and other urban infrastructure and services, 4.1%
Energy, 13.1%
Finance, 5.5%
Transport, 49.7%
Health, 7.1%
Industry and Trade, 6.7%
Public sector management, 4.5%

Share of RCI Loans and Grants in Total ADB 2021–2024
(Sovereign projects only)

	2022	2023	2024	2022-2024
RCI ($ million)	6,422	6,111	5,623	18,156
RCI (number)	46	45	38	129
ADB ($ million)	23,521	22,568	20,242	66,331
ADB (number)	184	178	165	527
% RCI ($ million)	27%	27%	28%	27%
%RCI (number)	25%	25%	23%	24%

ADB = Asian Development Bank, CWRD = Central and West Asia Department, EARD = East Asia Department, PARD = Pacific Department, RCI = regional cooperation and integration, SARD = South Asia Department, SERD = Southeast Asia Department.

Note: The information contained in Figure 29 is indicative at the time of writing and subject to change on the basis on future ADB operational programming.

Source: ADB.

Progress toward the next RCI corporate report. The next RCI corporate report is expected in 2024. It is expected to focus on the continued implementation of OP7 contributing to the end of the COVID-19 emergency, fair and equitable distribution of vaccines, strengthened regional health security, larger and more diverse collective action among countries, and tangible contributions to robust recovery in diverse cross-border flows that deliver wider socioeconomic and environmental benefits for everyone in Asia and the Pacific.

APPENDIX 1
ADB'S APPROACH TO REGIONAL COOPERATION AND INTEGRATION

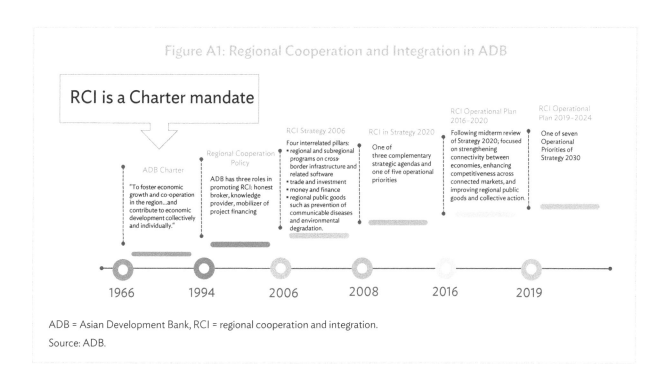

Figure A1: Regional Cooperation and Integration in ADB

ADB = Asian Development Bank, RCI = regional cooperation and integration.
Source: ADB.

Regional cooperation and integration (RCI) is a proven approach to foster development in Asia and the Pacific. RCI is vital for attaining national development goals, with cross-border infrastructure as the backbone of the process. Trade liberalization and foreign direct investment have been important in building global and regional value chains. Liberalizing financial flows has helped drive the changes, while regional public goods (RPGs) have mitigated environmental and regional health impacts, among others. RCI has become a valued development strategy and the United Nations recognizes it as an important tool to implement the 2030 Agenda for Sustainable Development.[1] The dynamic effects of RCI support development by creating cross-border goods and capital markets, achieving economies of scale in production, improving competition, increasing investment and jobs, catalyzing wider knowledge and technology dissemination, and jointly managing shared natural resources and mitigating risks to public health. The region's economic integration supports global economic progress.

---

[1]   F. Kapfudzaruwa et al. 2017. The Sustainable Development Goals and Regional Institutions: Exploring their Role in Asia and the Pacific. *Policy Brief.* 11. Tokyo: United Nations University.

The regional development approach stands as the crucial nexus between the national and global ones. RCI helps achieve complementarity, efficiency, and synergy at scale by coordinating and linking development planning and operations across neighboring countries, while adapting and customizing delivery of global knowledge and experience to inform regional and national development policy and programs. Studies confirm that RCI has had a significant and positive effect on the region's economic growth and helped reduce poverty. The dimensions of the regional value chain, movement of people, and institutional and social integration have been important in shaping economic growth. RCI appears to have provided significant opportunity to reduce poverty. The dimensions of trade and investment, money and finance, and institutional and social integration are drivers of poverty reduction. Their impact on curbing poverty is even more pronounced in lower-income countries. RCI across all dimensions appears to reduce poverty more than do efforts aimed only at individual dimensions.[2]

Notwithstanding the challenges to national development from the coronavirus disease (COVID-19) pandemic, the region continues to implement and develop trade and investment anchored in agreements, such as the Association for Southeast Asian Nations Economic Community, the Comprehensive and Progressive Agreement for Trans-Pacific Partnership, and the Regional Comprehensive Economic Partnership

Fostering RCI is an inherent strategic role and responsibility at the Asian Development Bank (ADB). The strategic importance of RCI is anchored in the ADB Charter.[3] ADB has gained a comparative advantage in RCI, using an approach tailored to the needs of different parts of Asia and the Pacific. The approach has pragmatically focused on projects that have built transport and energy connectivity between countries, improved trade and investment facilitation, supported high-quality technical studies and advisory work, and shared benefits and risk mitigation among participating developing member countries. ADB has carried out RCI mainly through four subregional programs: the Central Asia Regional Economic Cooperation, the Greater Mekong Subregion, the Pacific Islands Forum, and the South Asia Subregional Economic Cooperation. They provide platforms for ADB to plan and implement a substantial portion of its support for RCI in cooperation with countries and other development partners. The programs have three interrelated components: relationships, knowledge, and investment. ADB has three vital roles in RCI: (i) honest broker, serving as secretariat and convenor to ease policy dialogue and collective action among countries; (ii) knowledge provider and capacity builder, creating and disseminating knowledge, developing country and institutional capabilities, and advocating Asia and the Pacific RCI in global forums; and (iii) financier, mobilizing project financing.

ADB's Strategy 2030 advances RCI. Under ADB's Strategy 2030,[4] OP7,[5] RCI operations are expected to strengthen connectivity and competitiveness, promote RPGs, reinforce financial cooperation, and strengthen subregional initiatives. The objectives are achieved through (i) greater and higher-quality connectivity between economies, (ii) expanded global and regional trade and investment opportunities, and (iii) increased and diversified RPGs.

---

[2]   ADB. 2018. Regional Economic Outlook and Development Challenges. *Asian Economic Integration Report 2018: Toward Optimal Provision of Regional Public Goods in Asia and the Pacific.* Manila. pp. 12–14.

[3]   Article 2 (ii) of the Charter mandates ADB "to utilize the resources at its disposal for financing development of the developing member countries in the region, giving priority to those regional, subregional as well as national projects and programs which will contribute most effectively to the harmonious economic growth of the region as a whole, and having special regard to the needs of the smaller or less developed member countries in the region." ADB. 1966. *Agreement Establishing the Asian Development Bank.* Manila.

[4]   ADB. 2018. *Strategy 2030: Achieving a Prosperous, Inclusive, Resilient, and Sustainable Asia and the Pacific.* Manila.

[5]   ADB. 2019. *Operational Plan for Priority 7: Fostering Regional Cooperation and Integration, 2019–2024.* Manila.

Countries and ADB worked together to adapt OP7 to manage the pandemic. Although formulated and approved by ADB months before the onset of the COVID-19 pandemic, OP7 has supported innovation and countries' collective response to the pandemic and expedited the transition to medium- and longer-term recovery. Countries and ADB concurred that joint actions to combat the spread of the virus and to ensure that shared capabilities to detect and treat infected citizens were of paramount importance. Various RCI subregional platforms promoted the smooth flow of essential goods and services; infection surveillance, prevention, and control; and regional health security coordination, planning, and monitoring. ADB provided knowledge, technical services, and financing for crisis responses and trade facilitation, including support for sustaining small and medium-size enterprises' continued participation in regional and global supply chains. Countries and ADB seized opportunities during the COVID-19 emergency to introduce new digital technologies and harmonize procedures and practices to support the expansion of trade and multisector interventions to protect regional public health.

The implementation of OP7 will continue to innovate and evolve and remain highly relevant. RCI opportunities have emerged for "building back better"—and together—inclusive, innovative, and sustainable recovery in Asia and the Pacific. The region's post-COVID-19 recovery will depend on the development of broader and stronger-linked regional and national capacities for preparedness and resilience. Other opportunities for cross-sector and long-distance RCI are, for example, the development of networked e-commerce hubs. Countries should accelerate the implementation of the Regional Comprehensive Economic Partnership Agreement, one of the largest regional and multilateral trade agreements in the world. ADB, in cooperation with other development partners, will continue to assist the region through sustained engagement with RCI subregional platforms and individual countries.

APPENDIX 2
PROJECT INFORMATION SUPPORTING REPORTED REGIONAL COOPERATION AND INTEGRATION RESULTS IN DEVELOPMENT EFFECTIVENESS REVIEWS, 2017, 2018, AND 2019

Table A2.1: Development Effectiveness Reviews: 2017 and 2018 Results (Supporting Strategy 2020)
Level 2: Results Framework Indicators

	No. of PCRs or XARRs	Results Achieved[a]	Achievement Rate (%)[b]	No. of PCR/ XARR	Results Achieved[a]	Achievement Rate (%)[b]
	ADB Operations Overall			Concessional OCR Loans and ADF Grants		
Results framework indicator 1: Cross-border transmission of electricity (gigawatt-hours per year)						
2017	1	500	99	1	320	99
Bhutan: Green Power Development Project, 497 gigawatt-hours per year						
2018	2	12,000	96	2	12,000	96
Georgia: Regional Power Transmission Enhancement Project, 11.530 gigawatt-hours per year						
Nepal: Energy Access and Efficiency Improvement Project, 57 gigawatt-hours per year						
Results framework indicator 2: Cross-border cargo volume facilitated (tons per year)						
2017	3	2,456,000	100	3	909,000	100+
Tajikistan: CAREC Corridor 3 (Dushanbe–Uzbekistan Border) Improvement Project, 289,000 tons per year						
Papua New Guinea: Lae Port Development Project, 2,000,000 tons per year						
Viet Nam: Greater Mekong Subregion Kunming–Hai Phong Transport Corridor: Yen Vien–Lao Cai Railway Upgrading Project, 167,000 tons per year						
2018	2	6,660,000	100	0	-	-
Turkmenistan: North–South Railway Project, 6,200,000 tons per year						
Kazakhstan: CAREC Corridor 3 (Shymkent–Tashkent Section) Road Improvement Project, 460,000 tons per year						

- = no operations; ADB = Asian Development Bank, ADF = Asian Development Fund, CAREC = Central Asia Regional Economic Cooperation, OCR = ordinary capital resources, PCR = project completion report, XARR = extended annual review report.

[a] Results achieved are aggregate amounts of outputs and outcomes reported in PCRs and XARRs circulated from 1 January to 31 December of the year indicated. Satisfactory: 85% or above.
[b] Achievement rate is the percentage of results achieved in total planned outputs and outcomes as stated in reports and recommendations of the President for the same operations and eOperations and estimated by project teams.

2017 COMPLETED PROJECTS

- Four completed regional cooperation and integration (RCI) operations in 2017 were satisfactory (achievement rates more than 85%) for both RCI indicators (cross-border transmission of electricity and cross-border cargo volume facilitated).
- Under the Bhutan: Green Power Development Project, greater green power exports to India from a hydropower project in Bhutan increased cross-border transmission of electricity by 500 gigawatt-hours per year.
  - » The project included (i) implementation of the Dagachhu project—a 126-megawatt run-of-river hydropower plant—mostly to export to India, using existing transmission interconnection, and (ii) extension of the distribution network to connect 9,586 households to the grid and provision of off-grid solar power to 116 public institutions.
  - » The clean hydropower exported to India displaced hydrocarbon-based power generation, and the use of electricity in Bhutan displaced the use of firewood and kerosene in households.
  - » Revenues from power export can be allocated by the government to socioeconomic causes for a long time after the project loans have been repaid.
  - » The project's development impacts cut across ADB's strategic agenda: inclusive economic growth, environmentally sustainable growth, and regional integration.
  - » The Dagachhu project was recognized as Bhutan's first power public–private partnership (PPP) and the world's first cross-border project to earn certified emission reduction credits under the Clean Development Mechanism defined in the Kyoto Protocol. The PPP model demonstrated by the project has been replicated in two other hydropower projects, the more recent one being the Kholongchhu hydropower project with 600-megawatt capacity and estimated to cost more than $630 million.
  - » The off-grid solar power subcomponent used emerging technologies, including super-bright light-emitting diodes, lithium-ion batteries, and super capacitors as storage.
  - » The impact of expanding rural electrification was less indoor pollution, better quality of life, and more economic opportunities.
- Completed transport projects in Papua New Guinea, Tajikistan, and Viet Nam facilitated a total of 2.5 million tons of cross-border cargo per year.
  - » Central Asia Regional Economic Cooperation (CAREC) Corridor 3 (Dushanbe–Uzbekistan Border) Improvement Project *[project info can be provided if needed]*
  - » Lae Port Development Project [project info can be provided if needed]
  - » Greater Mekong Subregion Kunming–Hai Phong Transport Corridor: Yen Vien–Lao Cai Railway Upgrading Project [project info can be provided if needed]

Sources: Asian Development Bank (ADB) Independent Evaluation Department. 2018. *Bhutan: Green Power Development Project.* Manila; ADB. 2017. *Green Power Development Project in Bhutan: Project Completion Report.* Manila.

2018 COMPLETED PROJECTS

Two energy and two transport operations achieved above-target results for the two RCI indicators (cross-border transmission of electricity and cross-border cargo volume facilitated).

Two energy projects in Georgia and Nepal helped transmit a cumulative cross-border electricity volume of about 12,000 gigawatt-hours per year. The regional power transmission projects boosted the countries' ability to export electricity to neighbors and support regional power trade.

- **The Regional Power Transmission Enhancement Project in Georgia** aimed to improve power trade in the Caucasus by rehabilitating and improving 11 substations and constructing a new one (Khorga), which, together with other ongoing transmission investment projects, was designed to improve the reliability of the grid and the quality of power supply. Net power exports were expected to increase from 10% of domestic power generation in 2011 to 20% by 2019. The planned project outcome was a reliable, stable, and efficient power operating system that meets increasing demand. Although the project was not directly involved in importing electricity into Georgia, it has major implications for future transit and trade of electricity in the region. The Khorga and Menji substations are integral to increasing exports to Turkey of hydropower generated by the Enguri hydroelectric power plant. Similarly, the Ksani and Marneuli substations are integral to the electricity trade between Russia and Armenia.
- **The Energy Access and Efficiency Improvement Project** aimed to increase energy access, energy efficiency, renewable energy, and capacity building in Nepal. The outcome was reliable and energy-efficient power supply with increased access and operational efficiency in the project areas. The seven expected outputs were (i) 132-kilovolt (kV) transmission lines, substations, and capacitor banks; (ii) 33/11 kV primary distribution and switching substations; (iii) rehabilitation of Marshyangdi and Gandak hydropower stations; (iv) 11 kV feeders and related equipment in pilot areas; (v) countrywide delivery of compact fluorescent lamps; (vi) solar and solar–wind hybrid street light installation; and (vii) capacity building for PPP mechanisms distributing and implementing the component.

Two transport operations resulted in facilitating 6.66 million tons per year of cross-border cargo volume.

- **The North–South Railway Project** helped Turkmenistan develop an integrated and efficient railway system, improving its access to and the prospects for increased trade with neighboring Kazakhstan, the Persian Gulf countries, the Russian Federation, and South Asia. The project funded power, signaling, and telecommunications for about 288 kilometers (km) of railway between Chilmammet and Buzkhun, as well as track maintenance and safety equipment. Improved rail passenger transport will allow greater passenger mobility and easier access to markets and health and educational facilities. It will create jobs for train crews and railway workers. With the increase in passenger traffic, small shops and food outlets will be set up at the new passenger and freight stations.
- **The CAREC Corridor 3 (Shymkent–Tashkent Section) Road Improvement Project** aimed to help rehabilitate a road in Kazakhstan, a key section of a transport corridor connecting the Russian Federation, the Middle East, and South Asia. The project will improve 37 km of a four-lane, asphalt-paved road that runs from Shymkent, one of the major industrial cities in south Kazakhstan, to Tashkent, the capital of Uzbekistan. The project will strengthen regional cooperation and trade along CAREC Corridor 3.

Sources: Asian Development Bank (ADB) Independent Evaluation Department. 2018. *Regional Power Transmission Enhancement Project in Georgia: Validation Report*. Manila; ADB. 2018. *Regional Power Transmission Enhancement Project in Georgia: Completion Report*. Manila; ADB. 2018. *Turkmenistan: North–South Railway Project: Completion Report*. Manila, https://www.adb.org/sites/default/files/project-documents/43441/43441-013-pcr-en.pdf; and ADB. 2018. *Energy Access and Efficiency Improvement Project in Nepal: Completion Report*. Manila.

Table A2.2: Development Effectiveness Review: Results 2019 (Supporting Strategy 2030)
Level 2: Results from Completed Operations: Projects Contributing to Operational Priority 7
Results Framework Indicators

Pillars	ADB Overall			Concessional OCR Loans and ADF Grants		
	No. of Completion Reports	Results Achieved	Achievement Rate (%)	No. of Completion Reports	Results Achieved	Achievement Rate (%)
Cargo transported and energy transmitted across borders	1 PCR SOV: GMS Nam Theun 2 Hydroelectric (Lao PDR; energy)	$219,300,000	100	–	–	–
Trade and investment facilitated	3 PCRs	$237,434,000	100+	3	$237,434,000	100+
	SOV: Central Asia Regional Economic Cooperation Corridor 2 Road Investment Program (UZB) (transport)	$122,222,222				
	SOV: CAREC Corridor 1 (Bishkek–Torugart Road) Project 3 (KGZ) (transport)	$115,211,765				
	3rd project failed to deliver					
Regional public goods initiatives successfully reducing cross-border environmental or health risks, or providing regional access to education services (number)	1 PCR and 1 TCR	3	100	1 PCR and 1 TCR	3	100
	SOV: Second GMS Regional Communicable Diseases Control (CAM; health)	2				
	1 TA: Malaria and Communicable Diseases Control in the GMS (REG; health)	1				

– = no operations, ADB = Asian Development Bank, ADF = Asian Development Fund, CAM = Cambodia, GMS = Greater Mekong Subregion, KGZ = Kyrgyz Republic, Lao PDR = Lao People's Democratic Republic, OCR = ordinary capital resources, PCR = project completion report, REG = regional, SOV = sovereign, TA = technical assistance, TCR = technical assistance completion report, UZB = Uzbekistan.

Notes: 1. Results delivered as reported in PCRs, extended annual review reports, and TCRs circulated from 1 January to 15 November 2019. 2. 100+ achievement rate means that achieved results exceeded the planned results. 3. Achieved results more than 10,000 are rounded to the nearest 1,000. Values smaller than 10,000 are rounded to the nearest 100. Values smaller than 1,000 are rounded to the nearest 10. Values smaller than 99 are not rounded.

Source: ADB.

COMPLETED PROJECTS

- One completed RCI operation in 2019 (GMS Nam Theun 2 Hydroelectric) achieved the planned result for energy transmitted across borders amounting to $219.3 million.
- Two completed projects exceeded planned results, facilitating trade and investment amounting to $237.4 million.
- A completed project, the Second Greater Mekong Subregion Regional Communicable Diseases Control for Cambodia, and a completed regional technical assistance project, the Malaria and Communicable Diseases Control in the Greater Mekong Subregion, resulted in five RPG initiatives reducing health risks, achieving the planned results.

Table A2.3: Development Results from Completed Operations
(Sub-Pillars)—Tracking Indicators

Sub-Pillars	SDG	Results Achieved, ADB Operations Overall	Results Achieved, Concessional OCR Loans and ADF Grants
7.1.1 Transport and information and communication technology connectivity assets established or improved (number)	9	6	6
PCR: Road Network II			2
PCR: South Asia Subregional Economic Cooperation Information Highway Project			4
7.1.2 Measures to improve the efficiency and/or productivity of cross-border connectivity supported in implementation (number)	9	16	16
PCR: South Asia Subregional Economic Cooperation Information Highway Project	11		11
PCR: Central Asia Regional Economic Cooperation Corridor 2 Road Investment Program	1		1
TCR: Connecting the Railways of the Greater Mekong Subregion			1
TCR: Enhancing Coordination of the Central Asia Regional Economic Cooperation			1
TCR: Promoting Regional Knowledge Sharing Partnerships			1
TCR: Support for Pan-Beibu Gulf Economic Cooperation			1
7.1.3 Clean energy capacity for power trade installed or improved (megawatt equivalent), SDG-aligned SDG proxy indicator	9	1,000	–
PCR: Greater Mekong Subregion: Nam Theun 2 Hydroelectric		995	
7.1.4 Regional or subregional mechanisms created or operationalized to enhance coordination and cooperation among DMCs in energy, transport, or ICT connectivity (number)	17	1	1
TCR: Support for the Bay of Bengal Initiative for Multi-Sectoral Technical and Economic Cooperation II			1
7.2.1 Measures to improve execution of provisions in existing or new trade or investment agreements supported in implementation (number)	17	8	8
PCR: Second Investment Climate Improvement Program			6

continued on next page

Table A2.3 *continued*

Sub-Pillars	SDG	Results Achieved, ADB Operations Overall	Results Achieved, Concessional OCR Loans and ADF Grants
TCR: Enhancing Coordination of the Central Asia Regional Economic Cooperation			2
7.2.2 Measures to develop existing and/or new cross-border economic corridors supported in implementation (number)	17	3	3
TCR: Assisting the Central Asia Regional Economic Cooperation Institute Knowledge Program (Phase 1)			1
TCR: Enhancing Economic Analysis and South–South Learning			1
TCR: Supporting Industrial Park Development in the Central Asia Regional Economic Cooperation Region			1
7.2.3 Measures to improve regional financial cooperation supported in implementation (number)	17	2	2
TCR: Mekong Tourism Innovation			1
TCR: Support for South Asia Subregional Economic Cooperation			1
7.2.4 Regional or subregional mechanisms created or operationalized to enhance coordination and cooperation among DMCs in trade, finance, or multisector economic corridors (number)	17	23	23
TCR: Advancing Regional Cooperation and Integration through Brunei Darussalam–Indonesia–Malaysia–Philippines East ASEAN Growth Area, and Indonesia–Malaysia–Thailand Growth Triangle			2
TCR: Asia Pacific Public Electronic Procurement Network			3
TCR: Assisting the Central Asia Regional Economic Cooperation Institute Knowledge Program (Phase 1)			1
TCR: Building Capacity for Enhanced Connectivity in Southeast Asia			1
TCR: Central Asia Regional Economic Cooperation: Investment Forum			1
TCR: Greater Mekong Subregion: Capacity Development for Economic Zones in Border Areas			1
TCR: Implementing the Greater Mekong Subregion Human Resource Development Strategic Framework and Action Plan (Phase 2)			2
TCR: Improving the Performance of Labor Markets in the Pacific			1
TCR: Mekong Tourism Innovation			2
TCR: Promoting Regional Knowledge-Sharing Partnerships			1
TCR: Strengthening Compliance Review and Accountability to Project Affected Persons of Financial Intermediaries			1
TCR: Support for South Asia Regional Economic Cooperation			1
TCR: Support for the Partnership with the Emerging Markets Forum			1
TCR: Supporting Evaluation Outreach, Knowledge-Sharing, and Partnership Initiatives in Selected Developing Member Countries			5
7.3.1 Measures to improve shared capacity of DMCs to mitigate or adapt to climate change supported in implementation (number)	13	1	1
PCR: Enhanced Use of Disaster Risk Information for Decision Making in Southeast Asia			1

continued on next page

Table A2.3 *continued*

Sub-Pillars	SDG	Results Achieved, ADB Operations Overall	Results Achieved, Concessional OCR Loans and ADF Grants
7.3.2 Measures to expand cross-border environmental protection and sustainable management of shared natural resources supported in implementation (number)	12	–	–
7.3.3 Measures to improve regional public health and education services supported in implementation (number)	1	9	9
PCR: Second Greater Mekong Subregion Regional Communicable Diseases Control			3
TCR: Joint Control of Transboundary Animal Diseases in the People's Republic of China and Mongolia			1
TCR: Malaria and Dengue Risk Mapping and Response Planning in the Greater Mekong Subregion			2
TCR: Pacific Information and Communication Technology Investment Planning and Capacity Development Facility			1
TCR: South Asia Urban Knowledge Hub			1
TCR: Strengthening the Pension Fund Industry in the Asia-Pacific Region			1
7.3.4 Regional or subregional mechanisms created or operationalized to enhance coordination and cooperation among DMCs on regional public goods (number)	17	10	10
TCR: Joint Control of Transboundary Animal Diseases in the People's Republic of China and Mongolia			1
TCR: Mekong Tourism Innovation			9

– = no operation, ADB = Asian Development Bank, ADF = Asian Development Fund, DMC = developing member country, ICT = information and communication technology, OCR = ordinary capital resources, PCR = project completion report, SDG = Sustainable Development Goal, TCR = technical assistance completion report.

Source: ADB.

APPENDIX 3
SELECTED REGIONAL COOPERATION AND INTEGRATION LOAN, GRANT, AND TECHNICAL ASSISTANCE OPERATIONS VALIDATED BY ADB INDEPENDENT EVALUATION DEPARTMENT, 2017–2020

Bangladesh: Bangladesh–India Electrical Grid Interconnection Project, 2010 and 2013[1]

The project, approved in 2010 (with additional financing in 2013), was Bangladesh's first cross-border connection with India to bridge the gaps in energy-poor areas and to generate economic benefits for both sides of the border. The project constructed a transmission link between Bangladesh and India, which made available an additional 500 megawatts (MW) of power since 2013, easing Bangladesh's growing power crisis.

The project helped create transmission, interconnection, operation, and power-exchange agreements between Bangladesh and India. In March 2012, the Bangladesh Power Development Board signed (i) an interconnection agreement with India's central power transmission utility and (ii) a 25-year power purchase agreement with a government power-trading company in India to import 250 MW from India. In 2013, the first competitively tendered cross-border power purchase agreement for 250 MW was also signed in 2013 and supported by an ADB technical assistance project. Several power traders in India have since started to submit bids to sell an additional 250 MW to Bangladesh in anticipation of the end of the contract for 250 MW. Overall, the project made Bangladesh's power supply more available and sustainable and increased cross-border power trade between Bangladesh and India.

....

[1] ADB. 2017. *Bangladesh: Bangladesh–India Electrical Grid Interconnection Project: Validation Report*. Manila.

Table A3.1: Overall Ratings: Bangladesh–India Electrical Grid
Interconnection Project, 2010 and 2013

Validation Criteria	PCR	IED Review	Reason for Disagreement and/or Comments
Relevance	Relevant	Relevant	
Effectiveness	Effective	Effective	
Efficiency	Efficient	Efficient	
Sustainability	Likely sustainable	Likely sustainable	
Overall assessment	Successful	Successful	
Preliminary assessment of impact	Satisfactory	Satisfactory	
Borrower and executing agency	Satisfactory	Satisfactory	
Performance of ADB	Satisfactory	Satisfactory	
Quality of PCR		Satisfactory	

ADB = Asian Development Bank, IED = Independent Evaluation Department, PCR = project completion report.

Note: From May 2012, IED views the PCR rating terminology of "partly" or "less" as equivalent to "less than" and uses this terminology for its own rating categories to improve clarity.

Source: ADB IED.

Kyrgyz Republic: Second Investment Climate Improvement Program (Subprograms 1–3), 2015, 2016, and 2017[2]

The programmatic approach was to ensure (i) flexibility in building on the satisfactory performance of previous subprograms and in incorporating changes into the external environment in subsequent subprograms, and (ii) effective implementation of reforms (not just amendments in laws and regulations).

Subprograms 1 and 2 established the State Guarantee Fund (SGF) for small and medium-sized enterprises (SMEs) and the legal and regulatory framework for e-payments and mobile services. Under subprogram 3, the government piloted the Internet Payment Gateway project to enable online payments for key public services. Since its establishment in 2016, the SGF has been profitable and issued guarantees that provided partial security for SME loans. By the end of May 2019, the SGF had supported 845 entrepreneurs, of whom 28% were women, and SGF-secured SME loans had helped create 1,711 jobs. The result, along with the introduction of other innovative financing products for SMEs, such as financing of warehouse receipts, has increased SMEs' access to finance. All of the above demonstrates how upstream policy and institutional reforms are implemented downstream.

Aside from the SGF, the program helped establish the Project Development Support Facility under the Ministry of Finance, funded from state budget allocations ($1 million to $2 million annually in 2015–2018) to finance feasibility studies and transaction costs of potential public–private partnership (PPP) projects. The government signed three PPP projects during program implementation and announced tenders for an additional 15 PPP projects totaling $166 million on 1 January 2019. The first PPP agreement was signed between the Ministry of Health and Germany's Fresenius Medical Care Deutschland GmbH to organize hemodialysis services in Bishkek, Osh, and Jalal-Abad, creating 100 jobs. The other two PPP projects were for cinema rehabilitation and e-ticketing of municipal transport in Bishkek.

---

[2]   Independent Evaluation Department. 2020. *Validation Report: Kyrgyz Republic: Second Investment Climate Improvement Program* (Subprograms 1–3). Manila: ADB. https://www.adb.org/sites/default/files/evaluation-document/607066/files/pvr-692a.pdf.

The program helped the country (i) obtain its first credit rating and Generalized System of Preferences Plus status with the European Union (EU), (ii) streamline and expedite investment under the Investment Promotion Agency, (iii) introduce technical and vocational education training curricula in selected industries, (iv) modernize and operationalize four phytosanitary and three veterinary laboratories to increase the potential for exports of high-value and high value-added food products to the EU, (v) ratify the trade facilitation agreement and operationalize the National Trade Facilitation Committee, and (vi) approve the action plan to institutionalize an improved investor grievance mechanism.

Overall, the program was successful in establishing an enabling environment to increase private investment by increasing SMEs' access to finance, improving PPPs, setting the preconditions for better opportunities to export to the EU, and providing greater transparency in governance through the e-procurement system.

Table A3.2: Overall Ratings—Kyrgyz Republic: Second Investment Climate Improvement Program (Subprograms 1–3), 2015, 2016, and 2017

Validation Criteria	PCR	IED Review	Reason for Disagreement and/or Comments
Relevance	Relevant	Relevant	
Effectiveness	Effective	Effective	
Efficiency	Efficient	Efficient	
Sustainability	Likely sustainable	Likely sustainable	
Overall assessment	Successful	Successful	
Preliminary assessment of impact	Satisfactory	Satisfactory	
Borrower and executing agency	Satisfactory	Satisfactory	
Performance of ADB	Satisfactory	Satisfactory	
Quality of PCR		Satisfactory	See para. 42

ADB = Asian Development Bank, IED = Independent Evaluation Department, PCR = project completion report.
Source: ADB IED.

People's Republic of China: Yunnan Integrated Road Network Development Project, 2010[3]

Yunnan is a mountainous landlocked province in southwestern People's Republic of China. Its per capita gross domestic product was 55% of the national average; and it ranked third-lowest among the country's administrative areas. Its remoteness and lack of an efficient and effective transport system were obstacles to inclusive growth in Yunnan, as road connections were inadequate and so constraining growth in trade volumes. The project's border areas in Yunnan generated less than 1% of the province's international trade, reflecting a lack of high-quality border crossings and road connections. Of the existing border crossings covered by the project, only three were class I crossings. To meet demand, it was considered necessary to improve road quality and connections. The impact of

---

[3] Independent Evaluation Department. 2017. *Validation Report: People's Republic of China: Yunnan Integrated Road Network Development Project.* Manila: ADB. https://www.adb.org/sites/default/files/evaluation-document/387646/files/pvr-541.pdf.

the project would be enhanced regional integration and trade between Yunnan and neighboring countries. The outcome of the project would be improved accessibility between rural and border areas, and an improved regional transport network in Yunnan.

In 2010, ADB approved the $250 million project to develop an integrated road transport system that supports sustainable economic growth in Yunnan Province, part of the Greater Mekong Subregion. The project helped complete the national expressway system in the province and constructed a highway from Kunming, the provincial capital, to the Myanmar border. The project was planned and designed to alleviate poverty and promote regional integration through improved rural connectivity and accessibility. The project upgraded regional roads serving national borders; improved roads, road maintenance, and public transport services in rural areas; and strengthened local institutional capacity. Average travel time on project roads was reduced by at least 40% (travel time by road from Longling to Ruili was reduced from 4 hours in 2010 to 2 hours in 2016; average travel speed on improved local roads is increased from 10–20 kilometers (km) per hour in 2010 to 30–40 km per hour in 2016.

Table A3.3: Overall Ratings—People's Republic of China: Yunnan Integrated
Road Network Development Project, 2010

Validation Criteria	PCR	IED Review	Reason for Disagreement and/or Comments
Relevance	Highly Relevant	Highly Relevant	
Effectiveness	Highly Effective	Highly Effective	
Efficiency	Efficient	Efficient	
Sustainability	Likely sustainable	Likely sustainable	
Overall Assessment	Highly Successful	Highly Successful	
Preliminary assessment of impact	No Rating	Satisfactory	
Borrower and executing agency	Satisfactory	Satisfactory	
Performance of ADB	Satisfactory	Satisfactory	
Quality of PCR		Satisfactory	See para. 43

ADB = Asian Development Bank, IED = Independent Evaluation Department, PCR = project completion report.

Source: ADB IED.

Regional: Pacific Private Sector Development Initiative (Phases I and II)[4]

In 2007–2017, ADB provided $6.1 million to the program, which launched 276 subprograms, of which 93 had been completed as of 30 June 2017. Australia contributed $49.8 million and New Zealand $4.5 million. The program aimed to improve the business environment in Pacific island countries by promoting private sector development policies under ADB country partnership strategies.

....

[4] Independent Evaluation Department. 2018. *Performance Evaluation Report: Pacific Private Sector Development Initiative.* Manila: ADB. https://www.adb.org/sites/default/files/evaluation-document/370546/files/in19-18.pdf.

Over the 10-year evaluation period, the program published 17 private sector assessments to analyze and identify country private sector development strategies and reform programs, demonstrating how private sector development priorities and work programs can align with the agendas of recipient countries. The client satisfaction survey showed that Pacific developing member countries (DMCs) valued the program's flexibility, rapid response, and demand-driven approach, as 68% of respondents revealed that the program was their first point of contact when they needed assistance from donors for private sector development.

The program's work on access to finance can be grouped into (i) building blocks such as the delivery of a secure transactions framework and (ii) innovative solutions such as supply chain financing to strengthen the private sector. The program helped Pacific governments draft legislation on secure transactions and develop and implement online registries for the efficient registration of movable collateral and access to the registry by financial institutions. This has resulted in a 27% increase in secured loans on average by financial institutions across six Pacific DMCs from 2014 to 2016: the Federated States of Micronesia, the Republic of the Marshall Islands, Palau, Solomon Islands, Vanuatu, and Tonga. According to the leading nonbank financial institution in Solomon Islands, Credit Corporation, the time spent approving a loan was reduced to 1 day after adoption of the secure transaction framework, as preparing agreements was made easier and the need for government approvals eliminated. In agricultural supply chain financing, the program supported a financing facility for cocoa exporters in Solomon Islands and piloted a financing facility for vanilla bean growers in Tonga.

The program fostered business law reforms to help strengthen legal and regulatory frameworks. It advocated for state-owned enterprise (SOE) reform through a publication,[5] which provided in-depth, country analysis of SOE performance to measure progress and stimulate reform initiatives. In Solomon Islands, the technical assistance helped put the country's SOEs on a sustainable financial footing, resulting in a remarkable turnaround of returns on equity and assets. In Papua New Guinea, the program and the Office of Public–Private Partnership collaborated on supporting Papua New Guinea's Public–Private Partnership (PPP) Centre, which included assistance in developing an implementation strategy, a PPP project pipeline, a business plan for the center, position descriptions, and a project development facility concept note for the Port Moresby and Lae airports. The program updated the Port Moresby and Lae airports' PPP assessments, while the Office of Public–Private Partnership worked on supporting the PPP process. Similar early coordination—that is, coordination within ADB units before they work with government counterparts—could help ensure greater cohesion in ADB's policy approach and deliver better value for money for Pacific DMCs.

---

[5]   ADB. 2016. *Finding Balance 2016: Benchmarking the Performance of State-Owned Enterprises in Island Countries.* Manila.

Lightning Source UK Ltd.
Milton Keynes UK
UKHW051938310522
403814UK00011B/117